THE
SCIENCE
OF
FOOTBALL

THE MATH, TECHNOLOGY, AND DATA BEHIND AMERICA'S GAME

WILL CARROLL AND TYLER BROOKE
FOREWORD BY PETER KING

To my dad, Chris Brooke, for always being my biggest supporter.
—Tyler Brooke

Sports Publishing books may be purchased in bulk at special discounts for sales promotion, corporate gifts, fund-raising, or educational purposes. Special editions can also be created to specifications. For details, contact the Special Sales Department, Sports Publishing, 307 West 36th Street, 11th Floor, New York, NY 10018 or sportspubbooks@skyhorsepublishing.com.

Sports Publishing® is a registered trademark of Skyhorse Publishing, Inc.®, a Delaware corporation.

Visit our website at www.sportspubbooks.com.

10 9 8 7 6 5 4 3 2 1

Library of Congress Cataloging-in-Publication Data is available on file.

Cover design by David Ter-Avanesyan
Cover photo credit: Getty Images

ISBN: 978-1-68358-459-9
Ebook ISBN: 978-1-68358-460-5

Printed in the United States of America

CONTENTS

CONTENTS

FOREWORD

Not long ago, I was talking to a top NFL decision-maker, someone with the most power in his organization aside from the owner, about analytics. This person told me what his team was looking for in new football-intelligence employees.

"Someone smarter than we are, and someone who thinks different than we do," this decision-maker said.

So this person went to a brainy East Coast university to talk to grad students in several programs about football analytics, and to see if any of them would fit his organization. He explained how there was lots of data—from GPS tracking of players, to deeper statistical analysis of player performance, to managing player health by measuring high-stress markers during practice and games—his team wasn't sure it was using well.

He interviewed ten or twelve people, and asked three back for second interviews. Two were men, and they showed up in crisp business attire. The other was a woman. She didn't know much about football, wasn't a fan, barely had heard of this team. But in the second hour of the in-person interview, she suggested something (I don't know precisely what; analytics is a classified operation inside most NFL buildings) about the GPS data and performance that lit a light bulb above this decision-maker's head.

This team hired two of the interviewees, including the woman. I hear she's brought new ideas to the organization. When I hear the buzzword *analytics* about the NFL these days, I think of that.

But it's not just math/science brains changing the landscape in the NFL. It's people thinking differently. It's Nick Saban, at Alabama, hiring fired coaches for a season or two, while they're between jobs, to educate his staff and players about things like RPOs (run-pass option plays). It's then Eagles coach Doug Pederson empowering the coaches on his staff to think of better ways to run plays—and thinking of better plays, period. And listening to the coaches, with a no-good-idea-gets-left-behind mantra . . . the kind of philosophy that led to the winning play in Super Bowl LII.

Football is a smarter game than it's ever been. And I am going to tell you a story about one of the reasons it is.

Early in this century, a football nerd named Neil Hornsby lived in Luton, England, and he had a dream: What if I could organize a different way to look at football than is currently done? What if I could grade every player on every play of every game—with the kind of quality analysis that NFL executives and coaches would respect? He started this deep analytical look at games, but couldn't gain much traction in the NFL, in part because it took a long time to look at every play in a game twenty-two times, minimum, to judge how each player on the field did on the play. Plus, most NFL people didn't trust that Hornsby and his band of merry football freaks from all over the globe really knew the game well enough to know the assignments of every player. (Truth is, they don't. So Pro Football Focus was never meant to be flawless.)

By 2009, Hornsby was on the verge of giving it up. He couldn't find enough fans and teams to pay the bills. But he stuck with it another year, and one team, then two, then four started paying for snap counts and formation numbers and things like that. Hornsby was emboldened, and even when—as happened in 2011 when he toured some NFL training camps to try to drum up business—one GM thought some bloke with a thick accent could never know this distinctly American game and told him he had no interest in his numbers, Horsnby persisted.

In 2014, Cris Collinsworth, a huge PFF fan who used its stats and numbers in his weekly preparation for *Sunday Night Football*, bought a majority stake in the company. And in 2017, it was all worth it.

In Super Bowl LII, with the Patriots up 33–32 on the Eagles with

2:25 left, Philly had a third-and-7 at the New England 12-yard line. Nick Foles leaned into the huddle and called:

"Gun trey left, open buster star motion . . . 383 X follow Y slant."

The Eagles had flown to Minneapolis the previous Monday with 192 plays on Doug Pederson's Super Bowl play sheet. He'd told his staff the hay was not in the barn, and if you guys find a better play, I'll sub it in for one of the existing plays. Late on Monday night, in his Radisson Blu hotel room by the Mall of America, receivers coach Mike Groh found something. Groh was the offensive assistant assigned to study all "stacks and bunches" from every other game in the league. Groh noticed the Patriots having some trouble with Jet Motion—the sprint motion by a back or receiver pre-snap—and noticed they had trouble with stack formations too.

Groh used the database of Pro Football Focus to find every play that year the Patriots faced that sprint motion, and how they responded to four receivers overloading one side of the field. Groh wondered, *What if we did both on the same play*? He brought the idea and PFF evidence to offensive coordinator Frank Reich, who took it further up the food chain to Pederson. The head coach loved it. He put *Gun trey left, open buster star motion . . . 383 X follow Y slant* in the game plan. Groh's idea. Pederson loved how it would put tight end Zach Ertz alone—the Eagles thought—on Pats safety Devin McCourty with no help available.

The Eagles practiced it twice—that's it—during the days leading to the game. And with the season on the line in the Super Bowl, Pederson called it.

The sprint motion (Star Motion, in the Eagles' vernacular) worked perfectly and left Ertz on McCourty, one on one. No help. Foles hit Ertz. Touchdown. Eagles win.

What I love about that? The confluence of an invention by a Briton (Hornsby) who loved football, data, hard work, imagination, trust in a position coach and guts to call a newly invented play on the biggest stage of the year won a Super Bowl.

It won't be the last time data and new thoughts win a Super Bowl. That's one of the things that makes pro football so interesting right now, early in its second century.

—Peter King, 2022

INTRODUCTION

Smashmouth. Slobberknocker. Hog Mollies. Big Uglies. There's a ton of fun football terms that sound like exactly what they are. To the uninitiated, NFL-style American football—which we will henceforth just call "football" for ease, with apologies to the world game we'll call "soccer" here—is anything but scientific. It's big men smashing into other big men. George Plimpton once called football "violence punctuated by committee meetings." He wasn't wrong, but the game has evolved from a more violent and frankly more American game, into something that looks more like America in 2022. There's more technology, more complexity, and much, much more science in the game.

What we have tried to present here is the idea that the principles of science are woven into the fabric of the game in a way that is either invisible or taken for granted to such a degree that the science is ignored. Newton showed us that force is equal to mass times acceleration, but few of us do that equation when an edge rusher beats his man and bashes the quarterback, causing the ball to flutter out of his hands while his spine tries to deal with an unexpected trauma.

Football is not a game that innovates quickly. Ten years ago, the Super Bowl came to our town of Indianapolis and that game—Eli Manning's Giants over Tom Brady's Pats—was best known for the "helmet catch." I recently watched highlights of that game and it looks almost exactly like football does in 2022. Things have changed, to be sure, but those things are often not apparent to the most casual watchers . . . like the ones who show up once a year to watch the Super Bowl, or at least the commercials.

If we take it back to 2002's Super Bowl, we're met with the St. Louis Rams of Kurt Warner and—oh my—Tom Brady's Patriots.

That "Greatest Show on Turf" game was one of the legend makers for Brady and his brief flirtation with retirement reminds us that his career is an absolute outlier. When George W. Bush's dad flipped the coin at that Super Bowl, the season after 9/11, the US was in its first months of the "War on Terror" in Afghanistan and it hadn't yet reached Iraq.

Still, the game looked modern. There was more running, less passing, but it's not a far cry from what we see today. A land war in Asia came and went, while football just adjusted, a little bit and a little bit more, year after year. The game evolved towards a quarterback-dominated affair, forcing small adjustments to defenses, which led to more changes in offenses.

Helmets? Shoulder pads? Stadiums? All pretty much the same, then and today.

But just under the surface, there have been plenty of changes. The players have, as always, continued to get bigger, faster, and stronger. They've also gotten smarter, taken more control of their careers and their voices. From the broadcast you watch to the app you make a bet on, from the offense to the defense to the front office, the game of football is reliant on innovation, data, and even math for many of its innovations.

Material science? That'd be the lightweight shoes, the turf they play on, or the kevlar used in so many repaired joints.

Satellites and GPS? Yep, positional tracking for workload management, broadcasting the games, and even finding you to deliver a cold beer inside the stadium.

I could go on and on with examples of how science is at the heart of it, but I don't want to give away all the good stuff. That comes later, in these pages and in your imagination.

This isn't a textbook or a Football 101. There's going to be some basic terms and concepts that we simply don't have time or space to go over here. We think that the kind of person that picks up a book called *The Science of Football* is going to either already know those basics or be able to look them up and learn as we go along. We hope we'll neither lose you along the way nor insult your intelligence.

Just a glance at our table of contents tells you that we'll be covering a lot, breaking things down into a myriad of topics and subtopics. However, you don't need to read this front to back. Pick and choose according to your interests and your time. Rather than watching talking heads tell you what you just saw, grab this book and read about why it happened in the first place.

Writing a book is a tough task. We can't write about everything, so don't expect this to be exhaustive. Similarly, we have to choose where to plant our flag. It's a moment in time, here in 2022, and things will change. If you're picking this book up in 2042, you'll probably laugh at some of the things we thought of as "advanced," but I think, like looking back twenty years from now, the game will be both largely the same and nothing alike at all.

I doubt we'll have twenty-two robots on the field a few decades from now. I think the game will still be men, flawed and fragile but bigger, stronger, and faster, and also smarter. The game's evolution is part of its draw and this look at the science and technology underlying that evolution is, we hope, going to help the game by making fans smarter as well.

We're ready, so let's go to the playbook. In this case, Gus Malzahn's Auburn playbook from just a few years back. Believe it or not, the playbooks that teams hold so close during seasons often leak out and there are whole sites that have these available!

Huddle up tight with us, team. Second down and seven. Slant right Utah, Indy Back Zip, 52's the mike, on two. Slant right Utah on two. Ready? Break!

OFFENSE

Casual football fans are naturally drawn to the offensive side of the ball. It's the unit that usually scores all the touchdowns, produces most of the highlight plays, and generates the league's biggest superstars.

Since the Associated Press began awarding players the NFL MVP award in 1957, there have been only three years where an offensive player didn't win. It took exceptional, game-changing performances from Alan Page and Lawrence Taylor on defense to get recognized, and a consistent effort in a strike-shortened season from placekicker Mark Moseley in 1982.

NFL games have typically become high-scoring affairs in the modern era, but that wasn't always the case.

The earliest offensive innovations, including Knute Rockne's "Notre Dame Box," featured all eleven players bunched tight together near the line of scrimmage. Wide receivers and tight ends weren't even considered positions at the time.

By 1922, the first season of NFL statistics available on Pro Football Reference, the Canton Bulldogs won the league that year with a 10–0–2 record, averaging only 15.3 points per game.

The modern NFL offense is completely unrecognizable from its early days. Offenses have become more and more spread out, coaches have continued to innovate, players have become more athletic, and rule changes have favored the offense in recent decades.

The average NFL offense in 1922 scored 9.1 points per game. The league hasn't had teams scoring fewer than 20 points per contest since 1993, with 2020 featuring an all-time high in scoring with 24.8 points per game.

The way the modern NFL offense operates continues to change by the generation, but coaches have always emphasized the importance of blocking, regardless of the era.

Legendary Packers head coach Vince Lombardi stressed blocking when taking over in Green Bay with his implementation of the "Packers Sweep." The play was a simple handoff to the running back who tried to run to the outside of the formation to find open space near the sideline. Although the play sounded simple enough, it required constant practice and repetition for his offense to get comfortable with their assignments in order to achieve maximum effectiveness.

The left guard in Lombardi's power sweep was tasked with the most difficult assignment, pulling all the way across the formation to the other side of the field before having to read who to block based on the defense.

Lombardi turned the Packers Sweep into a science, relying on all eleven players executing as efficiently as possible. The play became a staple of Green Bay's offense, which went on to win five NFL championships over nine seasons.

Blocking schemes have evolved since the 1960s, but then again, so have the players, including the offensive linemen. As offenses have become more pass-heavy and more up-tempo, it has required offensive linemen to adapt to the times, becoming more athletic and agile. Future Hall of Fame offensive tackle Joe Thomas played in the league as this evolution was taking place.

A four-star recruit out of high school, Thomas stayed in state when he chose who to play for in college, committing to the Wisconsin Badgers. After seeing time as an extra blocker as a true freshman in 2003, Thomas became a full-time starter the next season, starting in every remaining collegiate game despite tearing his ACL as a junior in the Capital One Bowl.

After being named a consensus All-American and receiving the Outland Trophy as the nation's top interior offensive lineman, Thomas declared for the 2007 NFL Draft. Coming in at over 6'6" and 311 pounds, scouts were enamored with the talented prospect.

The Cleveland Browns selected Thomas with the third overall

pick of the 2007 NFL Draft. He spent his entire career with the team from 2007 until retiring in 2017. His accolades include six first-team All-Pro selections, ten Pro Bowl appearances, a place in the Cleveland Browns Ring of Honor, and certainly a future spot in the Pro Football Hall of Fame.

Thomas has stayed close to the game since retiring, working as an analyst for NFL Network and co-hosting *The ThomaHawk Show*, a podcast with his former teammate Andrew Hawkins.

Having spent a decade and a half around the NFL, Thomas has seen a shift in how teams, scouts, and coaches evaluate offensive linemen in today's league, and he took some time to share some of that insight with me.

"When I first got in the NFL, it was more about big, strong, physical offensive linemen," Thomas told me. "Athleticism wasn't that important because teams were running the ball more and quarterbacks were a lot less mobile."

Tall, imposing quarterbacks like Tom Brady and Ben Roethlisberger required more physical linemen, according to Thomas. When they were standing in the pocket, defenses would need to get through linemen quickly rather than going around them, because these quarterbacks would get the ball out quickly. With a different kind of passing game and fewer designed outside runs, offensive linemen simply needed to be bigger and stronger.

In today's NFL, that's no longer the case. Spread offenses, vertical passing attacks, and outside zone schemes are requiring more and more from their linemen, resulting in athleticism becoming a much more important factor.

Penei Sewell is a textbook example of the NFL beginning to value athleticism over size and strength. A standout tackle at Oregon, Sewell was listed at a little over 6'4" heading into the 2021 NFL Draft. Despite his shorter height for a tackle prospect, Sewell showcased some impressive athleticism in the pre-draft process with good scores in the broad jump and 40-yard dash.

Sewell was taken with the seventh overall pick in the 2021 draft and had a strong rookie season, starting 16 of 17 games for the Detroit Lions. Athleticism will help Sewell in his NFL career, but Thomas says it's not the only thing that makes a valuable offensive lineman in today's league.

"Smarts and consistency play a huge part," Thomas said. "As an offensive lineman, your value is the polar opposite of a defensive lineman."

Where defensive linemen and edge defenders are credited for tackles for loss, sacks, fumbles, and turnovers, offensive linemen are measured by their ability to prevent those things. Consistency plays a big factor in that, because even the best performance for a starting left tackle can quickly be derailed by allowing a strip-sack on your quarterback, with a defender causing the QB to fumble before they're able to get the pass away.

"A pancake block is cool, but it doesn't really impact the play much more than anything else when you're doing your job correctly," Thomas explained. "That's pretty minor compared to you whiffing your block and giving up a sack. That has a significantly bigger impact on the outcome of the game."

Media outlets and casual fans love to highlight pancake blocks, or blocks where a player is able to drive his defender into the ground, when watching offensive linemen. Pancake blocks were previously one of the few quantifiable ways people could evaluate the position. With the introduction of analytics, and companies like Pro Football Focus, it has changed the way the position is viewed and evaluated.

"Unless you played offensive line or were a coach that was heavily involved in the position, it can be hard to understand the value of an offensive lineman," Thomas said. "If they don't know how many times one player did their job correctly compared to another, or have any other way of evaluating linemen, then they're going to be much more influenced by the pancake blocks and other flashy plays a guy makes."

Teaching fans and media members what goes into playing on the offensive line is important for Thomas, and he feels like the analytics crowd has helped in a big way by highlighting the star linemen like Trent Williams and Zack Martin. While not household names to the average fan, Williams and Martin have begun to receive national recognition and All-Pro selections thanks to sites like Pro Football Focus providing player grades to show how dominant they are at their respective positions.

One of the ways Thomas feels that the evaluations and perceptions of offensive linemen are changing thanks to analytics is conceptualizing every play that they're involved in. An example that Thomas gives is offensive linemen previously being individually criticized when a defensive end had three or four sacks in a game.

"With today's data, you can contextualize that performance," Thomas said. "Instead of the offensive lineman receiving all the blame, you can show if a quarterback was holding onto the ball too long or scrambled out of the pocket, and whether the defender was rushing against a different blocker."

Another big shift in the way offensive linemen are utilized in the NFL has been the versatility of players. In the past, tackles may have never been considered to play elsewhere on the offensive line, and even moving from left tackle to right tackle was considered a big challenge.

That hasn't been the case in recent years. After being selected in the second round of the 2019 NFL Draft, Green Bay Packers offensive lineman Elgton Jenkins has played all over the offensive line. Since coming into the league, Jenkins has played at least one snap at all five positions on the offensive line, with most of his reps coming at both left guard and left tackle.

"I think that coaches are beginning to embrace [offensive line versatility] more," Thomas said. "They're understanding the importance of having your best five linemen on the field. Maybe it's an analytics thing, but finding guys who can play both guard and tackle can be really helpful heading into a week where you want to find the best five players that match up best with the defense you're about to be playing."

One of the biggest things that Thomas has noticed from his time as a rookie to now is how much more coaches use advanced concepts to make decisions, including the decision to go for it on fourth down.

"The risk-reward paradigm has shifted significantly, and coaches have started to lean into analytics, probability, and statistics." Thomas said. "Whether that's going for two or going for it on fourth down, the decision used to be much more about how coaches would defend the decision to their bosses and fan bases rather than relying on probabilities of success."

One of the big reasons fans didn't see more aggressive coaches was that they were much more risk-averse, according to Thomas. Whether it was avoiding media criticism or backlash from the fans, old school coaches were much more content with doing things the way they'd always been done.

"For a new coach, their job on a day-to-day basis is to avoid getting fired," Thomas said.

Changing Fourth Down

Fourth down used to be synonymous with special teams at all levels of football. It would signify the end of an offensive drive with a punt or field-goal attempt, except in rare circumstances of desperation for teams trying to come back from a large deficit with little time remaining.

The mentality surrounding fourth downs has changed entirely in the NFL. In 2021, the league saw an unprecedented number of fourth-down attempts, with teams going for it 793 times over the course of the regular season. Although the league had an extra week of games, there were 44.05 fourth-down attempts per week in 2021, significantly higher than in 2020, where there were 38.7 fourth-down attempts per week on average.

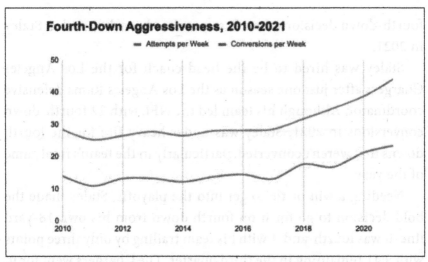

Fourth-Down Aggressiveness, 2010-2021

— Attempts per Week   — Conversions per Week

The evolution of fourth down in the NFL. *Graph by the author*

What was once viewed as a strategy for Madden video game players has been adopted by head coaches across all levels of football. Although analysis that shows specific game situations, both distance and game time dependent, to go for it on fourth are slowly becoming adopted across the league, perhaps no aspect of the game has been changed more by the adoption of statistical analysis than fourth-down aggressiveness.

Different statistical models have been created, and some adopted by NFL teams to make decisions in regard to going for it on fourth down. The *New York Times* has its own 4th Down Bot, while NFL's Next Gen Stats has its own algorithm to determine win probability based on decisions to go for it, punt, or kick a field goal.

There are multiple factors that go into these models that help coaches determine whether to go for it. Field position, distance from the first-down marker, time remaining, and the score all play into the decision from a mathematical perspective, but coaches will also consider matchups and momentum when making their own decisions.

Younger coaches in the NFL have begun to embrace going for it on fourth down, and no one was under more scrutiny for their fourth-down decisions than first-year head coach Brandon Staley in 2021.

Staley was hired to be the head coach for the Los Angeles Chargers after just one season as the Los Angeles Rams defensive coordinator. Although his team led the NFL with 22 fourth-down conversions in 2021, Staley was under heavy fire for the fourth downs that weren't converted, particularly in the team's final game of the year.

Needing a win or tie to get into the playoffs, Staley made the bold decision to go for it on fourth down from his own 18-yard line. It was fourth-and-1 with his team trailing by only three points with 9:41 remaining in the third quarter. The Chargers went for it, but running back Austin Ekeler was tackled for a two-yard loss, giving the Las Vegas Raiders the ball back inside the red zone. The Raiders kicked a field goal to go up six points and ultimately won the game in overtime to eliminate Los Angeles from a playoff berth.

"I understand the criticism. We felt like we could get the run," Staley said in his postgame press conference. "I understand that that decision will be questioned, but in my mindset that's a yard that we can get."

Despite media outlets hammering Staley's decision, NFL's own Next Gen Stats agreed with the decision. Per their model, the Chargers had a 1.4 percent higher chance of winning by going for it rather than punting.

Always Fight, Never Punt

Staley isn't the first coach to be aggressive on fourth down, and he certainly won't be the last. There might not be another coach across all levels of football who has drawn more attention to the fourth-down debate than coach Kevin Kelley, former head coach of the high school powerhouse Pulaski Academy known as "the coach who never punts."

Kelley started coaching back in 1993, but initially had no plans of ever becoming a coach. After graduating from college with a major in accounting, Kelley spent the first few years out of school away from football.

"My educational background might have been why I gravitated towards numbers early in my football career before I even knew what analytics was," Kelley said.

In his first year out of college, Kelley was an assistant manager at a clothing store, focusing on budgets, loss prevention, and staffing. With a little bit of luck, and a friend who was involved in coaching, he was able to find a junior high coaching job in Dallas, Texas.

Two years later, Kelley left coaching to help a friend run a golf retail store, where he became a part owner and used his accounting background to get the new store up and running. After helping get the store set up, Kelley sold his ownership back to his friend a year later to return to the coaching world.

In 1997, Kelley got the job that would define the rest of his football career. He accepted a role as offensive coordinator with Pulaski Academy, a private high school in Little Rock, Arkansas.

Kelley wasn't able to start calling the offensive plays his first two seasons with the Bruins. Coming into the job with an offensive philosophy that included a faster passing game with more wide receivers, the head coach at the time wanted to focus on personnel and formations utilizing fullbacks and frequently running the ball. Coach Kelley was finally able to develop his own system, call plays, and run his offense in 1999.

"I really didn't know a lot coming out of high school about football," Kelley said. "Since I majored in accounting instead of coaching in college, I had to do a lot of self-teaching to get acclimated and effectively coach at the high school level."

By learning the game of football on his own, Kelley was able to come up with his own unique strategies for running an offense, rather than learning from someone else. He focused on studying defensive coverages and viewing the field as quadrants of space where he could use his players to put stress on certain coverages in different parts of the field.

Kelley admits that his first season truly running the offense in 1999 was experimental by trying out different concepts and plays that he had yet to test in real game situations, yet the Bruins saw a lot of success. The team recorded over 3,000 yards passing that year, something that had never happened in Pulaski Academy's history.

The Bruins offense continued to evolve in the next several years. In 2000, Kelley's offense recorded over 5,000 passing yards. Then, in 2001, quarterback Thomas Thrash led the country and set a national record with 77 touchdown passes, throwing for 5,272 yards in the process.

Led by Kelley and Thrash, the Bruins made it all the way to the state semifinal, something that the school had only done twice in the history of its program. Thanks to the team's tremendous offensive success over his time as offensive coordinator, Kelley was named the school's head coach prior to the 2003 season.

It was here that Kelley began looking into a theory of his; what if his offense stopped punting? He had wanted to punt the ball less as offensive coordinator, but it wasn't until becoming head coach where he seriously considering eliminating the punt altogether.

Kelley started to ask his coaching staff to explain why teams punt the ball away. The answer he got was the same one used today, that punting the ball creates better field position for the defense, forcing the opponent to drive down a longer field in hopes of scoring a touchdown or field goal.

Coach Kelley wasn't convinced that field position mattered as much as it did, so he decided to try his strategy of rarely punting to give his offense an extra down to work with. According to Kelley, the Bruins punted just 21 times in 15 games, and the offense saw so much success that Pulaski Academy won its first-ever state championship in his inaugural season as head coach.

Over the next couple of years, Kelley would spend the offseason looking at the numbers his team generated from not punting, but also spent time evaluating himself. He soon realized that his play calling on later downs wasn't helping his offense as much as it could.

"It would be third-and-10, and my thinking would be that since my quarterback completes 65 percent of his passes, I'll just throw it twice and get the first down," Kelley said. "Instead I should have treated third down like it was second down, and take what the defense was giving us in order to make it a more manageable fourth down."

By 2007, Kelley's offensive strategy and fearlessness on fourth down began to attract the attention of national media outlets.

"There's a high school in Arkansas that has made the most significant football innovation we've seen since the veer option," Gregg Easterbrook, then of ESPN, wrote in November of 2007. "This high school is tearing up its state and is on the verge of revolutionizing the way football is played. In a copycat sport, Pulaski Academy of Little Rock has devised an offensive philosophy that is genuinely new, and it's winning games left and right. "

It wasn't until 2009 at the MIT Sloan Sports Analytics Conference where Kelley finally started to get a firm grasp of the data behind his ideas. As he networked with several speakers and attendees at the conference, he quickly realized that he was onto something that could change the way football is played.

Coach Kelley didn't want to completely surrender his decision-making to the numbers, however. He noted multiple times that he hates to admit it, but he does believe in what he calls "applied analytics," meaning that there are still certain moments in a football game where his situational awareness and in-the-moment strategy will trump the data.

"You have to know if you've been playing effective offense against their defense, but you can't just go by what's happening on the field," Kelley said.

Little did Kelley know that he had just hit the tip of the iceberg in terms of fourth-down analytics. He was asked to return to the Sloan Sports Conference in 2014, and during his time there he was able to reconnect with ESPN's analytics department. The network had compiled an extensive database of every snap that happened in college football, and Kelley bargained his way into spending an hour with their team to dive into the data.

With the biggest possible sample size at his disposal, Coach Kelley began to ask questions to attempt to quantify the psychology behind football. An example he mentioned was that he was interested in finding out what percentage of drives ended in a touchdown after a turnover vs a kickoff return at specific spots on the field.

"I was asking questions like that, and came away with some real answers," Kelley said. "Analytics was starting to take off in professional sports at the time, but up to that point it hadn't been able to penetrate into football."

Kelley's visits to the conference changed the way he thought about running his offense. He began looking into the routes his receivers ran, and which routes produced the highest yards after catch and missed tackle rates.

"Open field tackling is one of the hardest things to do at any level of football," Coach Kelley said. "I started looking at this data I was finding on different routes, and I started applying that to my passing game."

Along with his studying of routes, Kelley conducted his own study of his offense to see the impact that "drive-killing" plays like sacks and penalties had on their likelihood to score touchdowns.

While avoiding sacks and penalties isn't a new idea, Kelley optimized his offense to avoid these things entirely. He emphasized a quicker passing game from reducing the number of steps his quarterback needed to throw, to the depth of his receivers when attacking the field vertically.

Kelley shared some of the data that went behind his offensive optimization, based on self-scouting over a three-year period:

- When his starters were in, his offense would score on 88 percent of drives.
- If his offense had a penalty of any kind on a drive, they would only score on 14 percent of drives
- If a wide receiver dropped a pass that should have been caught, his team would only score on 12 percent of drives
- If the quarterback was sacked at any point in the drive, his team's touchdown probability on that drive dropped to 8 percent.
- If his quarterback could get the ball out 0.25 seconds faster per play over the course of 600 pass attempts, the offense would have 25 fewer sacks.

According to Kelley, in his first 15 years as a head coach, Pulaski Academy's offense ranked in the top 10 nationally in fourteen of those seasons. Once Kelley started self-scouting analytically in 2014, his offense took the next step, leading the entire country in offense in five of the next six years.

"We wanted to find a real-life way to eliminate sacks without compromising what we wanted to do on offense," Kelley said. "We didn't want to avoid sacks by being like the Pittsburgh Steelers, where Ben Roethlisberger was trying to get the ball out as fast as possible and limit the air yards of our passing game."

Kelley's entire philosophy for his offense started with the simple concept of being more aggressive on fourth down. Thanks to analytics, he was able to completely change the way he thought about calling plays, creating one of the most dominant runs of offense in high school football history.

However, the national debate about fourth-down aggressiveness continues to be divisive. Chargers head coach Brandon Staley was widely ridiculed on multiple occasions over the 2021 season for what was considered over-aggression on fourth down in certain games.

One game in particular where Staley came under fire was in Week Fifteen, with his Chargers falling to the Kansas City Chiefs in overtime after multiple failed fourth-and-goal situations in regulation. Los Angeles finished the game with five fourth-down attempts, converting on only two.

"I like [going for it] maybe once or twice, but I wouldn't say as many times as he went for it on fourth down," former NFL linebacker Rob Ninkovich said the week after the game on ESPN's *First Take*. "If you do that, you will lose. I know there's the analytics and computers of it, but I know that if you take the points, you win that game."

Fourth-Down Decision Analysis

Field Position	Distance (4th Down)							
	1 to 3	4	5	6	7	8	9 to 10	11
Own 1 to Own 31	Go For It	Punt	Punt	Punt	Punt	Punt	Punt	Punt
Own 32 to Own 42	Go For It	Go For It	Punt	Punt	Punt	Punt	Punt	Punt
Own 41 to Own 45	Go For It	Go For It	Go For It	Punt	Punt	Punt	Punt	Punt
Own 46 to Own 47	Go For It	Go For It	Go For It	Go For It	Punt	Punt	Punt	Punt
Own 48 to Opp 49	Go For It	Go For It	Go For It	Go For It	Go For It	Punt	Punt	Punt
Opp 48 to Opp 47	Go For It	Go For It	Go For It	Go For It	Go For It	Go For It	Punt	Punt
Opp 46 to Opp 38	Go For It	Go For It	Go For It	Go For It	Go For It	Go For It	Go For It	Punt
Opp 37 to Opp 35	Go For It	Go For It	Go For It	Go For It	Go For It	Go For It	Go For It	FG
Opp 34	Go For It	Go For It	Go For It	Go For It	Go For It	Go For It	FG	FG
Opp 33 to Opp 31	Go For It	Go For It	Go For It	Go For It	Go For It	Go For It	FG	FG
Opp 30 to Opp 28	Go For It	Go For It	Go For It	Go For It	FG	FG	FG	FG
Opp 27 to Opp 21	Go For It	Go For It	Go For It	FG	FG	FG	FG	FG
	Go For It	FG	FG	FG	FG	FG	FG	FG
	Go For It	Go For It	FG	FG	FG	FG	FG	FG

A commonly used "Go For It" chart, as posted on Reddit in 2020.

Coach Kelley believes that the fourth-down debate is over-blown, and that it was such a hotly contested topic on national media platforms simply because it was one that was easy to create controversy over. Considering how NFL teams have been more aggressive, and how many more fourth down attempts there have been in recent years, Coach Kelley may have a point.

"You can argue over it all day," Kelley said. "Analytically, Staley did the right thing [in Week Fifteen]. It's an easy argument on both sides, and everybody watching from the outside is going to have their own opinion."

The data continues to show that NFL head coaches are getting more aggressive with their fourth down calls, and Coach Kelley credits the younger coaches in the league for being pioneers on that front. Some of the most aggressive head coaches on fourth down in 2021 included Staley, Nick Sirianni, Matt LaFleur, Robert Saleh, and Kliff Kingsbury, all of whom have been NFL head coaches for three seasons or fewer.

Kelley noted that the resistance of older head coaches that he had known was mostly due to their belief in "gut feeling" over data from people who had never played the game. With football being a constantly evolving sport, he feels like the younger generation of coaches is turning fourth-down aggressiveness into the norm rather than the exception.

One of the big reasons Coach Kelley believes that going for it on fourth down is successful is that defenses haven't adjusted their mentality to defend against it.

"Defenses have been brainwashed for years that if they can get to third down, then they can get off the field with one play," Kelley said. "If a team is going for it on fourth down then you can't play defense the same way. You can't play the sticks on third down and give up anything underneath, because it's going to set up an easier fourth down attempt for the offense."

The mentality of fourth down, whether it's going for it or defending against it, has a real psychological impact on players, according to Kelley. With crowds getting louder and coaches buckling down, players who aren't used to the situation can perform differently.

Kelley cited a study of golfers to connect his point on fourth downs. In this study, Kelley says that golfers were randomly selected to attempt ten 10-foot straight putts to see how many they could make.

After attempting the putts, the same golfers were then asked to do the same trial but were offered $500 if they could make just as many as they had just made. The average number of putts dropped from seven all the way down to three when money was put on the line.

The study stuck with Coach Kelley, who began working on conditioning both his offensive and defensive players to get acclimated to crucial fourth-down situations. "You can get numb to anything," Kelley said. "Your mind is one of the most adaptive things in the world."

Kelley has been one of the biggest advocates at all levels of football for avoiding punts and going for it on fourth down. He firmly believes that it's the future of Division I and NFL football, but he feels that external factors are continuing to keep coaches from fully embracing it.

Job security tends to play the biggest factor in coaches being reluctant to be more aggressive on fourth down. Pressure from fans, owners, and particularly national media outlets can have a big impact on the decision-making, according to Kelley.

"The more accepting and less harsh the media is on coaches after the game, then the more I think coaches will be willing to embrace analytics," Kelley explained. "If they're going to continue to hammer coaches for making the right calls analytically and wrong calls traditionally, then I think it slows down the change."

At the NFL level, Kelley feels that more progressive ownership can help coaches embrace analytics as well. Owners who are more open to coaches like Staley being more aggressive on fourth down will allow them to make more analytically focused decisions without fear of losing their jobs, by Kelley's logic.

Kelley also said that he's talked to some of the biggest coaches in college football, and said that even the titans of the sport know that they should be going for it on fourth down. However, because of the pressure from fans, boosters, and athletic directors, they're not willing to risk losing their jobs.

"An athletic director can only back you for so long," Kelley said. "If you start making these decisions and they don't go the way the fans want them to, and they don't want to donate as much as they want to, then it becomes a problem."

Despite the external pressures that have kept football coaches from embracing his philosophies, Coach Kelley is still incredibly thankful to the fans of the game—not only because of their passion, but because of their knowledge of the game.

"It's the gift and the curse of football," Kelley said. "It can create negative emotions, but it can also bring people together more than anything else in this country right now."

It's unclear what the next step in Kelley's coaching career will be. He left Pulaski Academy to become the head coach of Presbyterian College, an FCS program, prior to the 2021 season. He led the program to back-to-back wins in his first two games by a combined score 152–46, with his quarterback setting an FCS record with 10 touchdown passes in the season opener.

However, the program proceeded to lose its remaining nine games of the season. Kelley announced after the season that he would be stepping down as head coach to "pursue other football interests."

Regardless of the next step in Kelley's journey, his offensive innovations at a private high school in Arkansas over the last twenty years have had a profound impact on the game of football at all levels.

Option Evolution

Innovation is a cornerstone of football, but not all innovation is the same. While some concepts have lasting impacts and fundamentally change the way the game is played, others become fads that fade away in a matter of years.

The 2008 Miami Dolphins are a perfect example of offensive innovation that took the league by storm, but couldn't last longer than a single season. After going just 1–15 the previous year, the Dolphins headed into their Week Three matchup against Tom Brady and the New England Patriots as 12.5-point underdogs with an 0–2 record.

Although the formation had been used in high school, college, and occasionally the pros before, head coach Tony Sparano and the Dolphins unveiled their "Wildcat" offense against the Patriots. With running back Ronnie Brown lined up in the shotgun as the quarterback, fellow running back Ricky Williams would come in motion from either side of the field and meet Brown at the point of the snap. Brown would then either hand the ball off, keep it himself to run, or occasionally throw a pass.

The Patriots had no answer for the Wildcat that day. On six plays out of the formation, the Dolphins gained 118 yards and scored four touchdowns on their way to a dominant 38–13 victory.

"We didn't have any idea that was coming," former Patriots linebacker Tedy Bruschi told ESPN in 2018. "I laugh at it now. But we were so pissed that day. I was hopping around. I didn't know what I was doing. It was a shock to the system."

After winning a single game the year prior, the Dolphins were able to win the AFC East for the first time in eight years thanks to the Wildcat formation, going 11–5 and making the playoffs.

Defensive coaches around the league spent the following offseason studying the Wildcat and figuring out how to defend it. Although the Dolphins attempted to continue running the formation in 2009, they didn't see nearly the same success, going just 7–9 and missing the playoffs.

Although the Wildcat has become an afterthought in the NFL today, there are parts of the concept that have remained. Perhaps one of the biggest recent offensive revolutions in football can be traced back to the Wildcat.

"You still see people use [the Wildcat]. I think the RPO thing came from that," former Patriots safety Rodney Harrison told ESPN in 2018. "Using a QB inside of a[n] RB to do that. People weren't afraid to use it as a surprise element in the NFL anymore."

The run-pass option, or RPO, is a concept that can be run from just about any personnel or formation. It's a simple concept, with a play being designed as a run play with the offensive line blocking as such. However, at least one wide receiver will also run a route during the play, and if the quarterback reads the defense and sees an opening, he will abort the handoff and quickly throw to his receiver.

The origin of the RPO is difficult to trace. Some credit former Texas high school coach Chad Morris for creating the RPO out of his triple option offense in the 1990s. Former Kentucky head coach Hal Mumme ran similar concepts in 1997.

"[In 1997 at Kentucky], we couldn't block Jevon Kearse, and so we told Tim Couch to either throw a bubble screen or hand the ball off," Mumme told *Banner Society* in 2018. "It was so easy to do. I don't know why we didn't keep doing it."

Other coaches credited with developing the RPO include former Michigan and West Virginia head coach Rich Rodriguez, former Louisiana Tech head coach Sonny Dykes, former Purdue head coach Joe Tiller, and numerous others. Even Hall of Fame quarterback Brett Favre has been given credit for running RPO concepts during his time with the Packers.

Regardless of who created the concept, the RPO has become a staple of college and high school offenses around the country, and even made its way into the NFL. According to Pro Football Focus, Power Five college football programs ran RPOs on 21.3 percent of their offensive snaps in 2020. The Minnesota Golden Gophers led the country with 48 percent of their offensive snaps being RPOs.

That number isn't as astronomical in the NFL, but there is a clear trend of growth. NFL teams attached an RPO to 6.1 percent of their plays in 2016, and that rate jumped to 8.6 percent after the 2020 season.

The 2016 season marked the first usage of RPOs to be recognized at a national level thanks to the Philadelphia Eagles. With starting quarterback and MVP frontrunner Carson Wentz suffering a torn ACL in the middle of the season, backup QB Nick Foles was tasked with taking over under center.

A backup quarterback would have doomed most teams with Super Bowl aspirations, but the work of head coach Doug Pederson, offensive coordinator Frank Reich, and QB coach John DeFilippo allowed the offense to keep moving thanks to the implementation of the RPO.

"I just think the RPO game is a unique way to put stress on different defenders," Reich told *USA Today*'s Doug Farrar in his book, *The Genius of Desperation*. "Usually, the stress you're trying to put on a defender [at the line of scrimmage] is to push them around. In the RPO game, sometimes that involves not blocking a defender and putting stress on him, like, 'Why is no one blocking me? What am I supposed to do? Should I run after the ball carrier or should I stand here and try to guard the receiver who's coming into this area?' That's some of the uniqueness of the RPO game, and when you get a quarterback who can read that unblocked defender quickly and deliver the ball with accuracy at different arm angles, it can be a very dangerous weapon."

The decision to implement more RPOs could not have worked out better for Foles and the Eagles offense. The backup QB completed 72.6 percent of his passes in the playoffs with six touchdowns and just one interception for a passer rating of 115.7. The Eagles went on to defeat the New England Patriots for their first Super Bowl victory in franchise history.

What makes the RPO so difficult on defenses is that it forces players to be in multiple places at once. For an unblocked defender, they can crash down to try and stop the run, but the quarterback can then abort the handoff and throw into his vacated area. If the defender stays back in coverage, then he takes himself out of the run play and the quarterback can just hand the ball off.

The concept becomes a matter of geometry for offenses, drawing up plays to find the right angles to attack defenses and put stress on key defenders. The play designs for RPOs are making things even harder for defensive coordinators to plan against, and analytics are backing that up.

Offensive efficiency can often be measured by EPA, or "Expected Points Added." It's a way of measuring how well a team performs over expectation, and can be measured on a per-play basis.

According to Pro Football Focus, the average run without an RPO added from 2018 through 2020 had a -0.117 EPA per play. When an RPO was attached to a run play, so the receivers were running routes as options downfield, that EPA per play jumped all the way up to 0.07.

EPA increased on passes with RPOs attached as well. For non-RPO pass plays to ones with the RPO attached, expected points added per play jumped from 0.064 to 0.110.

From an analytical perspective, the RPO brings significant value to both the running and passing games. Still, coaches across the NFL are hesitant to fully embrace the concept as a bigger part of their respective offenses. Where some college programs are running RPOs on nearly half of their plays, the NFL average is still less than 10 percent.

According to Mark Schofield from *USA Today*'s Touchdown Wire, the biggest reason for that has to do with the differences in downfield blocking rules between college and the NFL. In the NCAA, blockers are allowed to block within three yards of the line of scrimmage and still throw the football without drawing an illegal man downfield penalty. In the NFL, blockers are given just one yard of cushion.

"Put yourself in the mind of a linebacker at the college level," Schofield explained to me. "You see the quarterback extend the football to the running back in the backfield and there is a guard climbing towards you two or three yards downfield. You're instantly thinking about getting into a run fit because they're handing the football off, and you've got a guard to contend with. Yet once you climb downhill to meet the threat, the QB simply pulls and throws behind you on a glance route."

Because blockers must stay within a yard of the line of scrimmage during an RPO in the NFL, it gives linebackers significantly more time to read and diagnose the play before committing one way or the other. There isn't as much concern with committing to the run when a 330-pound offensive lineman isn't barreling downfield towards you immediately out of the gate.

The other difference could be in how college programs and NFL teams handle RPO concepts. Something that more savvy quarterbacks and coaches at the pro level will run are "pre-snap" RPOs, according to Schofield. In these concepts, the quarterback will usually commit to either handing the ball off or throwing a quick pass to the wide receiver before the ball is even snapped, based on the personnel, formation, and alignment of the defense. Fans often saw the Green Bay Packers run these kinds of concepts with Aaron Rodgers and Davante Adams.

"You might see more teams using pre-snap RPOs based on numbers like that," Schofield said. "But because of the blocking rules—and the differences between the NFL game and the college game in how downfield blockers are treated—the NFL might lag behind the college game still, despite the benefits to using RPOs."

They may not be used as often at the pro level, but the concept of RPO's has added yet another wrinkle that defensive coordinators are trying to find ways to slow down.

PASSING

Tom Brady. Joe Montana. Johnny Unitas. These legends of the game might not have existed if it wasn't for Walter Camp doing the unthinkable in the late 1800s.

American football looked much more like rugby during its inception than the game that fans watch today. In fact, the first recorded forward pass in the history of football didn't occur until Yale's Walter Camp threw one to Oliver Thompson for a touchdown against Princeton in 1879.

Princeton's players protested, but the referees ultimately decided to rule it a touchdown after flipping a coin. That play didn't immediately change the sport, however. It took nearly thirty years before the forward pass became legal.

John Heisman (you might recognize the name) was born in Cleveland, raised in western Pennsylvania, and came back to central Ohio to teach. Oberlin College isn't considered a football hotbed today, but it was where Heisman began his coaching career and ultimately started to establish his legacy.

"Mr. Heisman has entirely remade our football," The *Oberlin Review* wrote about him in 1892. "He has taught us scientific football."

Heisman brought several innovative changes to the game as a coach. He invented the flying wedge, the safety, but most of all, he made players like Brady and Manning possible thanks to the legalization of the forward pass.

When Heisman first witnessed a forward pass at a game between Georgia and North Carolina in 1895, the play was illegal. North Carolina's punter passed the ball downfield for a 70-yard touchdown, and despite protests from the Bulldogs, the play stood after the referee claimed that he didn't see the ball being thrown.

Heisman became enamored with the idea of the forward pass and began pushing the college football rules committee to legalize the play. After three years of pleading to the committee, the forward pass officially became legal in 1906, eventually paving the way for the stars of today.

The passing game has evolved over the past century-plus. Even the football itself has been changed to make it easier to throw. Once the forward pass became legal in the early 1900s, the ball was given a more aerodynamic shape to make it easier to throw. Although the ball has continued to evolve since then, the physics and aerodynamics behind throwing a football have stayed the same.

There are two main components to the physics behind a forward pass: the ball itself and the act of throwing the ball. Few people are more qualified to talk about these things than an established physics professor, regardless of their football background.

Stephen Schuh is a senior lecturer of physics and science division chair at Ball State University. He has been teaching at Ball State for 22 years with nearly three decades of experience teaching physics. Schuh provided me with an impromptu physics lesson on the forward pass to explain what makes throwing a football so unique compared to other sports.

Unlike a baseball, a football is much more dependent on angular momentum instead of pure velocity in order to successfully be thrown. "The key is that nature really wants to preserve momentum," Schuh said. "Which is why if you try to throw a football without a spiral, it's a nightmare."

As a football is being thrown in a certain direction (or vector), the ball keeps the same orientation as it is rotating in order to avoid losing velocity as well as its spiral. The example Schuh uses to explain this is rifling a barrel in a gun in order to make sure the bullet spins when the gun is fired. If the bullet doesn't spin, then the accuracy is completely lost.

"Any time you want something to be stable you put a spin on it,"

Schuh explained. Along with the spin of the ball, Schuh says that air friction plays a big part on the ball's speed. In order to explain the differences in a football, Schuh started with a baseball.

When a baseball is thrown without any spin (a knuckleball, for you baseball fans) air is typically moving above and below the ball at relatively the same speeds, causing high drag and the characteristic random flutter of the pitch. However, when spin is introduced on a baseball, air is hitting one side of the ball much faster than the other side, creating drag and causing the ball to drop or create movement like with a curveball or slider.

For a football, the way air friction hits it is completely different. Where a baseball's rotation will meet the air head-on, a football will be spinning on a perpendicular axis from the air. As the ball goes forward, its spin is going to the side.

This difference in how a football deals with air friction is likely a big reason why rotations per minute, or RPM are measured for quarterback prospects prior to the NFL draft. The data behind spin rate is becoming more widely available as well.

At the 2022 Shrine Bowl and 2022 Senior Bowl, Zebra Technologies provided data on all the quarterbacks participating in the week of practices, including spin rate. The average throw with a tight spiral from an NFL quarterback will have about 600 RPM. On the first day of Senior Bowl practice, Pitt standout Kenny Pickett produced the highest spin rate of the day at 674.2 RPM.

For a casual fan, rotations per minute on a pass may seem like nothing. However, according to Schuh while discussing friction on a ball, it's a significant factor.

"You're actually reducing friction on the ball the faster you spin it," Schuh said. "The faster spin rate actually helps create a partial vacuum around the ball, reducing its friction through the air."

Schuh also points out that spin rate on a ball may not have a drastic increase on the velocity of a pass, but that it would certainly reduce the friction it faces and improve the ball's stability over a longer distance. While the physics behind the ball itself are much different than baseball, the physics behind the act of throwing the ball are quite similar.

In the simplest of terms, the act of throwing a football relies on torque, or the rotational equivalent of force. Where force is generated in a straight line, torque is the way to angularly accelerate an object.

You may remember the formula "force equals mass times acceleration" from high school. Torque is simply force applied at a distance in a static situation. In the human body, the moment of inertia has to be factored in along with the biological properties of the motion, according to Dr. Michael Sonne with ProPlayAI.

Sonne also explained that torque produces a rotation of a segment about a joint.

"If you have two segments, where equal force is applied at an equal distance, the distal aspect of that segment will be moving tangentially faster on a longer segment (think Kyler Murray vs Josh Allen)," Sonne explained to me. "If you have two segments that are equal in length and distance of force application, but one segment weighs more than another, if you want them both to rotate at the same speed, a greater force will need to be applied in the bigger segment.

"At the end of the day, it all comes down to getting the distal aspect of the kinetic chain to move as fast as possible. There's a lot of ways to do that—more force, better kinematic sequencing, better deployment of the arm."

The moment of inertia signifies a resistance to acceleration. This is calculated by taking into account the mass and the distance from the rotational axis. For a quarterback, this would be looking at the size of their arm and the length of the arm from the shoulder joint that acts as the axis.

"Most people don't think of the quarterback as one of the big guys until they're standing next to one," Schuh said. "Because they

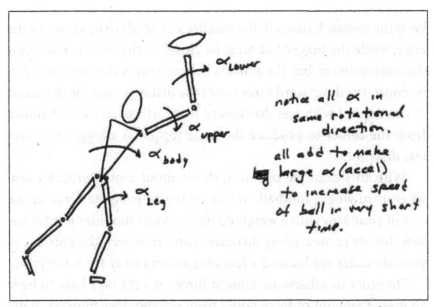

Handwritten notes in figure:

α_{Lower}

α_{upper}

α_{body}

α_{Leg}

notice all α in same rotational direction.

all add to make large α (accel) to increase speed of ball in very short time.

No one loves whiteboards like coaches and physicists. *From Steven Schuh.*

typically have both long and strong arms, they're going to have much higher resistances to acceleration."

The acceleration component is calculated by the difference in initial velocity and final velocity over time. For a quarterback, that's the time from starting the throwing motion to the ball leaving his hand. With NFL quarterbacks typically doing that in less than half a second, their angular acceleration, or "alpha" is also very high.

Compared to the average person throwing a football, an NFL quarterback produces much greater acceleration of their arm as a result of generating much more torque, producing a greater throwing velocity.

"If your alpha number is big and your inertia number is big, then your torque has to be monstrous," Schuh said.

Because NFL quarterbacks produce so much torque on their throws, the risk for injury is also significantly higher, especially to their shoulders. In order to explain this properly, start off by thinking about kids playing on a seesaw.

When a smaller kid is on a seesaw with a bigger one, in order to keep the seesaw balanced, the smaller kid needs to be closer to the edge, while the bigger kid must be closer to the center. You know this instinctively, but the science behind this is that for torque to be equal, the downward force times the distance must be the same. A smaller kid with less downward force will need more distance from the center to produce the same torque as a bigger kid with less distance.

With this example in mind, think about a quarterback's arm when throwing a football. While trying to generate force at the end of your arm with a weighted object, your shoulder joint is the axis that we're measuring distance from. However, the muscles in your shoulder are located a few centimeters away from the joint.

"In order to achieve maximum force on a throw, I have to have an insane amount of force going from my shoulder muscles to my joint, because that distance is extremely small," Schuh said. "As a rough example, if my arm is one meter long and my muscle is three centimeters from my joint, then I am producing thirty-three times more force on that small area than the force being applied to the ball."

This is just a very base-level introduction to the physics of the forward pass, and with more time Schuh would gladly go deeper into the details. Still, these basic physics concepts are instrumental to understanding what goes into throwing a football, and some have made a career out of using these concepts to improve throwing mechanics while keeping quarterbacks healthy.

House Call

Tom House is considered the godfather of modern pitching biomechanics, and although he primarily worked with pitchers in baseball earlier in his career, his work with quarterbacks has been instrumental in prolonging the careers of some of the most noteworthy QBs in the modern NFL era.

Before he was ever a coach and trainer, House was a pitcher in Major League Baseball, playing with the Atlanta Braves, Boston

Red Sox, and Seattle Mariners in the 1970s. While he was never a superstar in baseball, House had a respectable career. His most notable career highlight, however, was catching Hank Aaron's record-breaking 715th home run in the bullpen while playing for the Braves.

After retiring from baseball, House wanted to get into coaching. He ended up signing a ten-year deal with the University of Southern California, where he spent five years as a coach and the entire ten years as a researcher. His research included work on velocity improvement, biomechanical efficiency, and recovery.

House acquired a 3D motion analysis system to begin diagnosing how pitchers were throwing the ball. Instead of relying on video and the eye test, House was able to look at things he usually wouldn't be able to.

"You can see probably about 34, 32 frames a second," House told GQ.com in 2020. "But most of the activities with a quarterback or pitcher that count take place in about 1/250th of a second."

Although he had no intentions at the time, this work eventually led House into doing the same for quarterbacks.

In 2021, House told *Sports Illustrated* that he started to capture the throwing mechanics of prominent quarterbacks, including Dan Marino and Joe Montana, simply to collect as many data points as possible.

"We got a bunch of quarterbacks on the computer because, at that time, we were using a football as a training device," House told *Sports Illustrated*. "It was a great cross-trainer because it was heavier than a baseball, so it would build strength, and you couldn't throw a football wrong and make it spiral."

While House did little with this kind of data on quarterbacks initially, his breakthrough with elite quarterbacks came when the San Diego Chargers hired him to help with Drew Brees. While the role was initially meant to help Brees psychologically—House's doctorate is in psychology—that changed drastically when the star quarterback suffered a torn labrum and partially torn rotator cuff in his throwing shoulder in the final game of the 2005 season.

What started as a job working on helping Brees be less timid and more commanding in the huddle turned into a physical rehabilitation for House to help the future Hall of Fame quarterback be able to throw a football again. Once Brees was healthy, the focus was to sustain his throwing ability through something called biomechanics.

Like many in his industry, House's focus on developing his quarterbacks relies on biomechanics. While that may sound like an overly complicated concept, it's merely the study of physics applied to the human body. In House's line of work, his goal is to analyze biomechanics using motion capture technology to get his quarterbacks and pitchers to throw as efficiently as possible.

One of the ways that House and his team are able to analyze throwing efficiency is through something called kinematic sequencing, or the order and speed in which each body part accelerates and decelerates. House would analyze a QB or pitcher's throwing motion starting with the legs, then hips, shoulders, and arm.

One interesting example that House gave to GQ.com on kinematic sequencing came in the early 2000s, when they were collecting motion capture data on Brees and Hall of Fame pitcher Greg Maddux. When analyzing their kinetic sequences at 1,000 frames per second, the two were identical outside of timing and weight shift despite playing different sports.

Biomechanics are just one part of the performance equation, according to House. When clients come to work with him, he will also have them work on strength training, nutrition, and mental/emotional work to ensure that they're reaching peak performance.

For quarterbacks in the NFL, every small change can pay dividends in the game of inches. Every QB at that level, even the backups, got to the professional level for a reason, but the great ones are the ones who are always trying to improve.

"At (the NFL) level, they are all pretty good," House told *Sports Illustrated*. "Sometimes a two or three percent improvement can make a huge difference." House said. "It isn't just mechanics that we work on."

When an athlete works with House, he is put through a series of tests and evaluations to look at the player's timing, kinetic sequencing, and then things that coaches teach such as posture, stride momentum, and hip and shoulder separation.

Using Brees as an example again, House noticed through these evaluations that the quarterback's base was too wide, and that he was struggling to generate enough momentum from his front foot when throwing. Working with Brees to narrow his base, the goal was to increase the energy going into the football, allowing for a better long ball.

When working with elite athletes, House's intention isn't to fix what isn't broken. Instead, the goal is to continue making small adjustments so that these top-level players in their sports can make the most of their talents.

"These guys were really good before they showed up," House told GQ.com when talking about his clients. "So what we did is fixed small things, so instead of being 92 percent efficient, they're sneaking up on 97 to 98% efficient. And now that's long-term health and performance."

At the time of his shoulder injury in 2005, it was thought that Brees might never play football again. Thanks to House, Brees went on to play for fifteen more seasons with the New Orleans Saints, leading the NFL in passing yards in seven of those seasons while helping lead his team to the promised land as Super Bowl XLIV MVP.

With the success House had with Brees, other quarterbacks quickly reached out to work with the former MLB pitcher. This led to the creation of 3DQB, a biomechanics training company that has worked with most NFL quarterbacks, dozens of college QBs, and hundreds at the high school level. House partnered with Adam Dedeaux, the son of legendary USC baseball coach Rod Dedeaux, whose name is on the field where 3DQB started. Together, they quickly became known as the source for top quarterbacks in need of a tuneup.

House isn't afraid to celebrate this fact, either.

"We're pretty good. Like, real good," House told *The Guardian* in 2016. "We can tell you what you are today and tell you that if you do this with your legs, this with your torso, this with your arms as far as conditioning is concerned and do the same with the vectors of your body, then in six to twelve weeks you will be throwing this hard. That's why we keep having people show up."

3DQB and House have worked with multiple Super Bowl champions, All-Pros, and future Hall of Fame quarterbacks. However, none of their clients are as prominent as Tom Brady.

Around 2012, Brady began working with House to fix some mechanical issues with his throwing motion and delivery. Although Brady had been named MVP in 2010, the Patriots hadn't won a Super Bowl since 2004, and as the ultimate competitor the QB was looking for any way to improve and sustain his performance as he entered his mid-30s.

What House noticed when he began evaluating Brady was that his mechanics and kinetic sequence looked great except for the front side of his body was too low and was leading too quickly on throws.

The fix for Brady was to keep his front hand over his front foot and to keep it close to his face, or as House would explain it, "take a bite out of whatever burger you have in your hand."

"If you look at all the quarterbacks when they throw, it looks like they're taking a bite out of their front hand," House explained to GQ.com. "It's basically keeping all of your energy going in one direction."

Something else that House noticed was that Brady was

consistently missing high and low, but not side-to-side. In his experience, House knew that this would be a front-side elbow and arm thing. If Brady had been missing left and right, then it would be an issue with him moving his head.

"[House] says when you pass a certain age you really got to learn to re-learn," Tom Brady told the *Los Angeles Times* in 2012. "A lot of it's re-learning different things that maybe you've done, or have become habits that you've done thousands and thousands of times, (and) that you really need to train yourself a different way to improve certain aspects of your mechanics."

What House has done for quarterbacks has allowed some of the elite players like Brees and Brady to play well into their 40s, something that would have been unheard of just a few decades ago.

"We're in a perfect world right now where the technology is allowing people to identify stuff that's never been seen before," House said. "The next piece of the puzzle after identification is solution, and that's where we have a head start, because we started our science in the mid-'80s."

As proud as House is about the work he's been doing, he tends to shy away from some of the titles that have been given to him such as "the quarterback whisperer" or "pitching guru."

"That's their description, I'm just a coach."

QBs Go Mobile

For as much emphasis as the NFL has put on passing, perhaps the most noticeable trend among quarterbacks across the league has been the rise in the number of QBs who are mobile and athletic.

Players like Lamar Jackson, Kyler Murray, Russell Wilson, and Josh Allen have changed the way the position is being viewed, at least at the pro level. While most of these quarterbacks still rely on their efficiency as passers to help win football games, their athleticism and mobility has added an extra dimension to their respective offenses.

The NFL's perception of mobile quarterbacks changed forever when Michael Vick entered the league.

The number one pick in the 2001 NFL Draft, Vick turned heads immediately with his ability to improvise and scramble downfield. In 2006 he became the first quarterback in NFL history to rush for over 1,000 yards, and at the time of writing he holds NFL records in career yards per carry (7.0) and career rushing yards for a QB (6,109).

Vick had proven in the early 2000s that having a mobile quarterback could change the way coaches thought of a traditional NFL offense. The Baltimore Ravens took that and ran with it when they drafted Lamar Jackson in 2018.

Ravens general manager Ozzie Newsome was criticized at the time for taking Jackson in the first round. Former Colts GM Bill Polian was one of Jackson's harshest critics, making multiple public statements thinking that the Heisman Trophy-winning quarterback should move to wide receiver.

"He's short and little bit slight," Polian said on ESPN's *Golic and Wingo* in 2018. "Clearly, clearly not the thrower that the other guys are. The accuracy isn't there. So I would say don't wait to make that change [to wide receiver]. Don't be like the kid from Ohio State [Terrelle Pryor] and be 29 when you make the change."

There was plenty of opposition to those critics wanting Jackson to play wide receiver, however, including Vick.

"He's a quarterback," the former Falcons QB told NFL.com in 2018. "I've been hearing about things about him playing receiver, they'll probably say he needs to play defensive back next," Vick said. "But listen, the kid is 6-3, 215 pounds. But for anybody to say Lamar Jackson is a receiver, I don't think they understand the quarterback position. I don't think they appreciate the value that could be [brought] from the quarterback position."

Jackson started his first NFL camp behind former Super Bowl MVP Joe Flacco, but still ended up playing in all 16 games and starting in seven of them as a rookie. In those seven games as a starter, the Ravens went 6–1, and head coach John Harbaugh began to see a clear path on how to utilize his dynamic young quarterback.

Prior to the 2019 season, Harbaugh and offensive coordinator Greg Roman met and watched film with Paul Johnson, one of the masterminds behind the triple option offense that he ran with both Navy and Georgia Tech. The triple-option is traditionally a very heavy run offense with little passing, featuring tight ends and fullbacks in motion with multiple handoff and pitch outlets for the quarterback.

While the Ravens didn't plan on running the triple option as their base offense, they were looking to find ways to utilize their quarterback's exceptional speed and athleticism.

"We're sometimes teaching, always learning and we have a chance to learn and ask a lot of questions and to expand what we're doing," Harbaugh said after meeting with Johnson. "[Johnson] is a great football coach, obviously, and had amazing success over the years, both at Navy and Georgia Tech. Very unique offense."

By working with coaches from less-than-traditional offenses, the Ravens integrated some run-focused concepts into their offense. The results could not have been better for Jackson.

The second-year quarterback was named the NFL MVP, going 13–2 in 15 starts with 36 passing touchdowns and six interceptions to go along with an NFL record 1,206 rushing yards for a quarterback and seven rushing touchdowns while averaging 6.9 yards per carry.

Jackson isn't the only mobile QB of his time. Buffalo Bills quarterback Josh Allen has become a mobile threat in a completely different way than Jackson. While Jackson possesses blazing speed with a lengthy and thin frame, Allen has become a bruiser of a runner for Buffalo, coming in at 6'5" and nearly 240 pounds.

Through his first four NFL seasons, Allen has averaged more

than 100 rushing attempts per year. On 422 carries during that time, he's rushed for over 2,300 yards with 31 rushing touchdowns.

There are some who disagree with the Bills utilizing their franchise quarterback as a runner, however, largely due to their concerns over injury.

"He's more like Cam Newton but with a bigger, stronger arm," Tampa Bay head coach Bruce Arians told the *Buffalo News* after playing the Bills in 2021. "We talked about the designed quarter-back runs are tough. I wouldn't put my quarterback in that much harm's way because he did get nicked up a little bit."

The same criticisms were thrown at the Ravens in 2021 for their handling of Jackson. The star quarterback suffered an ankle injury in December and missed the final four games of the season.

Criticism over utilizing mobile quarterbacks isn't new and is a debate that continues to linger as the league adds dynamic playmakers like Jackson and Allen. However, the data may suggest that quarterbacks who run the ball more are in fact not more likely to miss games.

Looking at quarterbacks with at least three rushing attempts per game since 2000, we can also look at the percentage of games those players missed compared to the number of games in each season. While situations such as illness and poor play might have resulted in players missing games, a sample size of more than 5,000 games played should still give us enough statistical significance to see if mobility causes more injuries.

The results provided on the following page may be surprising for those who believe mobile quarterbacks are more often injured.

The trend line shows a negative correlation between availability and rushing attempts. It's worth noting, however, that this could be skewed in part due to the age of the league's top rushing QBs. Of the five players with the most rushing attempts per game on this chart, four of them were 25 years old or younger immediately following the 2021 NFL season.

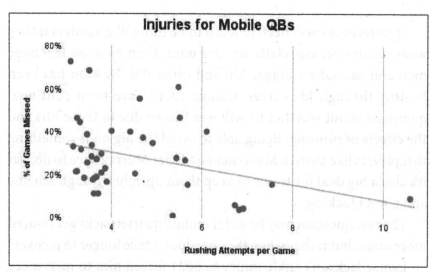

Injuries for Mobile QBs

Data shows mobile QBs are less likely to miss games. (Data 2000–2021, chart by authors).

Since 2000, only Lamar Jackson, Josh Allen, Kyler Murray, Cam Newton, Jalen Hurts, and Michael Vick have averaged more than six rushing attempts per game during their career. Vick is the only one of those players to have exceeded the "expected" percentage of games missed, in large part due to a broken leg he suffered in 2003.

There are many misconceptions about mobile quarterbacks. Simply being mobile doesn't equate to being "injury prone." Being mobile doesn't necessarily open up a quarterback to more injuries, according to the data. It's simple to see what does—getting hit. In most cases, a pocket passer with bad blocking (hi, Andrew Luck!) will be hit more than a scrambler, who is by definition avoiding contact. Think back to Barry Sanders, who was the ultimate shifty runner. He was short with a low center of gravity and amazing footwork. It seemed he could squirt through a tiny hole in the line and break something big while never taking a big hit. He'd get tackled, but never one of those highlight hits that makes the crowd go "ooh!" He was seldom slammed down or even knocked backwards. He was very healthy and is one of the few older players you'll see moving well years after his retirement.

Quarterbacks will need to learn to be more like Sanders if they want to survive, especially smaller ones. Cam Newton is a huge man and can take a bigger hit, and often did. Newton has been healthy through his career, though there have been continual questions about whether he will wear down due to those hits and the effects of running. Being able to avoid the big hit is something that players like Patrick Mahomes and Kyler Murray have to do, but it's also a big deal for teams to keep them upright through scheme and good blocking.

The real question may be not if mobile quarterbacks get injured more often, but rather when they do, does it take longer to recover?

Lamar Jackson's ankle injury in 2021 forced him to miss more time than the team originally anticipated. Dealing with a bone bruise, there was hope that he could come back for the end of regular season, but a video from practice went viral in late December that showed him limping at practice.

"There was a thought—and even with Lamar, Lamar felt he was going to be back," Ravens coach John Harbaugh said in his end-of-season press conference. "First week, he thought he had a chance. Second week, he assured me—he said, 'I'll be back, I'll be back.' He worked really hard at getting back. But it just didn't really heal."

Kyler Murray went through a similar process in 2021 when dealing with a sprained ankle. Jay Glazer reported during a *FOX NFL Sunday* broadcast that Murray could avoid missing any time with his injury due to it occurring on a *Thursday Night Football* game, giving him more time to rest.

Instead, Murray ended up missing three consecutive games with the injury. While it's impossible for anyone on the outside to know exactly why it took so long for Murray to get healthy, it would be understandable for the Cardinals to have wanted to be patient with their star quarterback until he was able to be a threat with his mobility once again.

Carroll believes that the major difference in these injuries compared to other QBs in the NFL is based almost entirely on that mobility.

When a quarterback is injured, he has to heal and get back to his normal level of functionality. For mobile quarterbacks, that includes being able to move. He can't just be able to drop back and stay stationary like a more classic pocket passer. Ankle, foot, and knee injuries will take longer to return from for a mobile quarterback because they simply can't be as limited and play their normal game.

A mobile quarterback will take longer to return, but not heal in most cases. A mobile quarterback could take six weeks or more to return from a high ankle sprain, whereas a less mobile quarterback could come back in less time since they only need a stable base. Teams switch to more shotgun snaps to take the load off this.

We saw the latter during Super Bowl LVI, when pocket passer Matthew Stafford dramatically limped to the sidelines after having his ankle rolled up. The athletic trainers worked hard to get him taped up over his shoe, and he was back out for the next series. It was checked for tightness throughout the game, but he had no further functional issue. On the other side, Joe Burrow twisted his knee, something the Bengals later acknowledged was an MCL sprain. It limited his lateral mobility and he ended up sacked more, including the Aaron Donald near-sack that ended the game.

Injuries can be that important, perhaps deciding games (as you'll see in a later chapter). For a mobile quarterback, there's just more moving parts in their movement.

Mobile quarterbacks aren't going away. In 2021, twenty-four quarterbacks who made a regular season appearance averaged at least three rushing attempts per game. Seven of those twenty-four averaged at least six rushing attempts.

NFL scouts and front offices used to treat athleticism in quarterbacks as an afterthought. Now, with the rise in mobile quarterbacks and run-pass option plays, head coaches and offensive coordinators have even more ways to make their passing games dangerous.

Trends in the NFL come and go, but the beginning of the twenty-first century has shown teams that having a superstar quarterback is essential to long-term success.

DEFENSE

At the most basic level, defensive football comes down to a couple principles. There is no "immovable object" just as there is no irresistible force. Instead, science has decided that there are three key things that defense must do, based on physics, psychology, and mathematics.

The first principle is purely Newtonian. A defense must be an equal and opposite force to the offense, within its strategic and philosophical constructs.

One of the most basic defenses, one you'll likely only see at youth levels, is called the "Gap 8" or "GAM" (Gap, All Man). There's no art to this one. Eight defensive players line up in each gap, between the offensive linemen and at the end of the line ("edge").

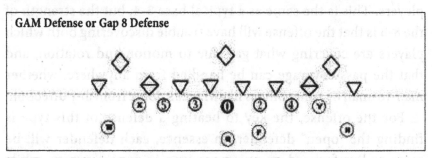

GAM Defense or Gap 8 Defense

The Gap 8 defense. *Diagram by author. 0 is the offensive center.*

The Gap 8 works because each gap is covered by a single man and in theory, one should be unblocked and the point of attack should be covered. Even a simple QB sneak, going between the gaps and over the center, shouldn't have any real success, keeping every play very simple. Success here comes down to execution; if all defensive players cover their gaps, it should succeed.

However, there are plenty of ways to beat the simplest Gap 8. Beating a single man at the point of attack breaks the entire defense.

A more complex blocking scheme, such as traps and sweeps, cause issue. Even a fullback lead blocking can cause issues. The Gap 8 is just too simple for all but goal line situations and even there, modern defenses go three-dimensional, putting in high and low calls for the various gaps, running linebackers into position to confuse and potentially attack the attack point with greater force or numbers.

For years, the Gap 8 has been all but unworkable at all but basic levels, but since the 1980s, some coaches have tried to use the principles of the Gap 8 and disguise it. One of the most successful Gap 8 variants is used in Texas, where Cedar Park's Joe Willis designed a defense that is both simple in principle but almost inscrutable to read. Called the 8-3, Willis's variant reverses the normal down lineman-linebacker code (3-4, 4-3 and so on) and is instead defined by the eight non-linemen, linebackers, and defensive backs.

Willis's variant uses three down linemen and eight standing players. This is the same as a typical base 3-4, but the strength of the 8-3 is that the offense will have trouble discovering both which players are covering what gap due to motion and rotation, and that the pass coverage can be handled from anywhere, whether man-to-man or zone. Blitzes likewise can come from any direction.

For the offense, the key to beating a defense of this type is finding the "open" defender. In essence, each defender will be more or less focused on one man, even in zone coverage, while one ends up heads up on the quarterback. Accounting for designed quarterback runs, this is ideal and allows for convergence. However, proper offensive play design and play calling can expose this open defender. Forcing that player to make decisions or move around can lead to mismatches. That player could be drawn in by play action with a route going just behind him, if the safety help is drawn away.

The 8-3 is simple enough in that the three down linemen are rushing predetermined gaps, with one of the linebackers becoming the edge rusher. The three remaining linebackers can do any combination of blitz, run blitz, man cover, or zone cover, along with the remaining four standard defensive backs. This is a lot of possibilities, but is easy to grasp from the defensive side.

However, the 8-3 does have weaknesses. A spread offense or wide line spacing can cause trouble maintaining gaps. Motion and shifts can expose the defense, especially in man coverage. The 8-3 almost always leaves at least one gap unprotected and a play that finds that weakness is guaranteed some yardage, if not a big play.

That leads us to a further variant, which doesn't really have a standardized name. Brian Flores, recently the head coach for the Miami Dolphins, used a version he called the "amoeba" while he ran the defense for New England. The "amoeba" had no set front, with only one down lineman. It was very difficult to read, but also required personnel that could conceivably do one of three things— defend the run, blitz, or defend the pass—and that personnel is difficult on a small 53-man roster. Despite its success, the amoeba hasn't been widely adopted and Flores seldom used it in Miami, nor did the Patriots continue its usage.

In Arizona, Vance Joseph has taken it a step further, removing down linemen altogether and essentially running an 0-6-5 scheme.

New England Patriots lined up in "amoeba" with one down lineman. *Video via NFL's GamePass.*

Joseph's scheme is the most extreme and is only used in long-yardage situations. It is designed to give the running play enough success to be tempting, but not enough to gain a positive advantage or a first down. There's a "bend but don't break" philosophy to many of these, but the real underlying principle is to make the least productive path the most apparently attractive. A defense is willing to give up a weakened matchup that leads to three yards, but not when it could lead to thirty.

The second principle is that a defense must not be simple to understand, at least from the offense's standpoint. Offenses spend time watching film, mapping tendencies, and even take time before each snap to identify sets and shifts in order to assign blocking and even change plays. Just as offenses like the run and shoot are based on figuring out which player is uncovered, the defense seeks the same, all while deceiving both the players on the field and the coaches as to their intent.

In 2019, Sean McVay's Rams went to the Super Bowl based on a spread concept, looking for gaps and reads to find spacing. (They returned to the Big Game in 2022, which suggests that defenses haven't quite figured this out!) Quickly, defenses adjusted, going to even more six and seven defensive back sets. Almost all of these are known as "hybrid sets," because they essentially become two halves that should work together—one is in the coverage and the other is in the rush. Rushing three isn't going to get to the quarterback much, leaving even doubled receivers a chance to find their way to an opening or seam. Even with seven or eight defensive backs, usually at least one will add to the rush with a blitz component.

The third is that the defense has to be able to adjust in order to maintain a sustainable failure rate. For the offense, they want to gain just over three yards per play, though many coaches will say four for a margin of error. Simply, the math works. Gain three and a half yards on every play—no more and no less—and an offense would score on every possession, assuming no penalties.

This obviously doesn't happen. Offense and defense move in fits and starts, with big plays on either side driving the ball in spurts. The old "three yards and a cloud of dust" simply doesn't work in practice, but the math of necessary gains still does. Attempting to pass for six yards carries the risk that the pass will be incomplete and gain zero, or worse, lead to a sack. The modern offense and defense has adjusted to this, increasing completion percentages, designing plays for yards after catch, and on the defensive side, shifting priorities depending on situation.

Coaches on the offensive side have long had down-and-distance charts on their play cards. For the defensive coaches, context is everything and it's a lot more than down or distance. Time remaining, offensive strengths, personnel, and score are the main components, but it's far more than instinctual. Every team in the NFL has done major simulations on what's to be expected in each situation, which leads to a risk tolerance/risk management approach to defense.

AI is turning this on its head. Using complex mathematical models, then outputting it into quick-check charts and Madden-like video, the data becomes easily usable and teachable. The addition of virtual reality and soon, augmented reality, will give defenses new weapons in terms of repetition and recognition.

One of the key outputs is to the very formations and positioning of players on the field. Since there's no real time communication possible, at least in a format that's usable by the entire team rather than the one designated player at the NFL level, most use a "best fit" and allow the player's reaction and vision to determine where they can go. More teams are now using models to tweak this—moving a player a yard here, a foot there—in order to have a better fit for the anticipated plays. The downside is that it does complicate calls and can actually shift players negatively, making things worse rather than better.

So far, most teams have gone to visual signals, often card

systems with ridiculous-looking symbols, like cartoon characters. An NCAA defensive coordinator, who was not authorized by his school and staff to discuss their signals, explained that he and most places use a similar system with varying codes. "Play, direction, and set is what we use, so three cards," he explained. "Play is what we anticipate is coming—run, pass, option, etc. Direction is just that, where we think it's going—right, left, center, deep. Set is our defensive positioning, which is partially set by personnel, but we'll shift the nickel, nickel hybrid, and coverage."

While the jargon can make this sound more complicated and the complex yet silly card-coding complicates it further, it's a relatively simple system with only a few adjustments. It's still hard to figure out that something like "Z Mo One Slot Check Yuma" is a simple zone defense, looking to rotate one linebacker to the strong side while covering the flat and curl zones for short yardage. This design, a key of the 2013 Seahawks' "Legion of Boom" defense is predicated on simple principles with nearly endless variations. However, it's seldom used today because its design is in part reliant on accounting for a fullback, which is used much less frequently in recent NFL offenses.

It's in all these ways—seeing a defense go from the very basic "ours against yours" kind of heads-up defense to a computer-modeled defense with no defined positions, all measured based off analytics, that we witness the true evolution of the game over the years. That evolution is accelerating as we go from players getting bigger, stronger, and faster to computers doing much the same, as well as the speed of getting from input to decision.

You'll often see offensive concepts come in as lightning strikes, catching defenses off guard. The "Wildcat" offense, with its quick sweeps and direct snaps to the runner, confused the reads of most defenses and created a speed lane almost exactly where the hesitation would occur. The downside was, the offense wasn't very complex and defenses quickly adjusted. The Wildcat is less an offense and more a gimmick, one you see used on occasion.

Game Speed

One of the most interesting applications of both "next generation stats" and computer modeling is a true understanding of what coaches have long called "game speed." This isn't a difficult concept—how fast can a player move in-game? At its most basic, it is merely the speed and velocity, both peak and sustained, that a player can generate. A faster player will outrun a slower player in most situations, but the game isn't quite that simple.

The NFL's "Next Gen Stats" are basically location-based and allow looks into actual game speed in certain situations. An NFL quality control analyst—a coach that basically watches films and grades each player's performance after games—told me that what he looks for on these outputs isn't top speed, but burst. "It's much like what we look for at the combine," he says, "but it's in game. We can see when a runner is looking for a hole and then explodes out. We can see who can get the angle and chase someone down. We can see who gives up on a play early or takes one off when it goes to the other side."

Coaches have for years relied on subjective or poor measures of speed. Forty-yard dash times don't have much application to a real football game, but watching film or games and saying "that guy looks fast" is even less accurate in most cases. The type of location data available now is clear, but what to do with it remains an issue. One NFL defensive coordinator at the NFL Combine told me that while he looks for peak speed, others in his profession disagree. "So much of peak is when it happens," he explained. "If you have to be in the open field, like a wide receiver who gets behind someone, well, that comes up once or twice and it doesn't take a data scientist to figure out that kind of fast." He told me that burst is what he'd really like to know, but there's no good metric yet that gives him that.

Finding that burst—the ability to accelerate to speed quickly—is more important to defenders than pure top speed. "My [defensive back] comes out of a cut, or gets turned around. How fast is he back on his guy?" asked the coordinator. "I have to watch tape for that now and I'll probably always have to do that to get his instincts. Or a linebacker that waits, waits and then reads the play and shoots a gap. That's the speed I want and it's almost all burst."

That leaves defensive coaches and quality control coaches with their hands full with tape, judgments, and trying to make sense of whatever data they have available. It's very early days for the ability to make truly informed decisions, but that's not to say that what these coaches aren't doing isn't data-driven. It's just a very informal basis, a subjective rather than an objective basis.

An NFL quality control coach told me that there are things he can look at on tape that speak to speed, but have nothing to do with speed per se. "One of the things one position coach wanted from me was who was near the ball on a tackle. Not in on the tackle, but near. Then he wanted to know who came from defense left (left as the defense looks forward) and was near the tackle defense right, or vice versa," he explained. "So the weak backer got all these points for not making a tackle, but the middle two (linebacker, in a 3-4 set) came off slow. They didn't get to the play from pursuit, as he wanted. I never thought it meant they were actually slow and when we looked back at the end of the season, there wasn't any correlation to things like peak speed or even 40 times when we looked back."

However, this kind of judgment and "old-school film work" is a part of football at the upper levels. The QC coach reminded me that the position coach was recently promoted to a defensive coordinator position. "He's moving up," he told me, "and so I bet he's going to do that again, whether or not it really correlates. There's a new crew learning his methods, so it gets perpetuated until someone wins with something more objective."

One of those objective systems being used is positioning. The systems are often referred to as GPS (global positioning system, like the navigation system in your car) or LPS (local positioning system, for indoor or domed stadiums, which use fixed beacons rather than relying on satellites.)

It's all good information, but where it's really becoming useful for defensive coaches is in figuring out positioning. The QC told me that his team's coaches are getting input from data analysts and computer modelers based on those speeds. "Say I have a guy with great everything, but he's a step slow at linebacker. If we can cheat him a step or two in the right direction, he's suddenly a step or two faster, or at least that's how it will feel to the runner."

These models are getting increasingly complex and increasingly proprietary. "We don't even show the players," the QC said. "They could get cut. They could get traded. They just know where we move them. Some of them figure it out," he said laughing.

The downside of these models is that they have to assume an offensive play. Shade a guy a step or two the wrong way and now he's effectively slower, not faster, and perhaps unable to get in on a play. There's both geometry and physics to consider. Speed can overcome a slight disadvantage, but there's speed at every position in modern football. One step, one slightly wrong pursuit angle, and all a defender is going to see is the back of the guy going the other way.

Since positioning data is still relatively new to the league and almost impossible to get at lower levels, there's still a gap to optimizing its usage. Analysts focused on both sides of the ball are working to find those small advantages, and the first to do it will have one of the few asymmetric advantages left in football. My guess, sitting here in 2022, is that it comes no later than 2025 and creates such an advantage that we'll see a "dynasty" formed from it, where that first team will have a two to three win advantage over the competition until the rest figure it out, adjust, and catch up.

Leverage

If speed versus speed determines many matchups, strong versus strong naturally decides others. But it isn't just the strongest player or team that wins, otherwise we'd just dead lift to decide the winner. Instead, the techniques of football, along with the system of offense or defense, use the physical principle of leverage to help players win at the point of contact.

The simplest application of this is "low man wins," a truism for lower-level coaches, teaching blockers to get their pad level (shoulders, usually) low and to force their opponent to stand up, putting them in a weaker position and allowing the "low" player to move them more easily. Unfortunately, this doesn't always work and techniques and even plays have been designed to exploit this. The famous "over the top" dive, ubiquitous in the 1970s, is the answer to a goal line battle of linemen trying to get low. When they zig, you zag, right?

Beyond this, leverage and technique comes down to intent. Do you want to keep someone in place, or turn them to one side? Do you want to drive them back or knock them down? Do you want to lock on or disengage? Can you simply run around them or through them?

For defenders, especially edge rushers as have evolved in the post–Lawrence Taylor era, a series of techniques designed to disengage, redirect, and accelerate have become a basic part of the arsenal. Swim moves, spin moves, and hundreds more are practiced on both sides of the ball, an artful ballet of violence. While strength and speed are key, it is often the most technical execution that wins. An unexpected spin move or a drop step against a blocker's timing can create an easy win at that point, hopefully blowing up the play.

This is the reason that technique is such a key and focused on so much on both sides of the line. According to Matt Jones, the run game coordinator and offensive line/tight ends coach at UT Martin, there are three key principles to leverage—leverage of the body, leverage of the hands, and leverage to the point of attack.

Leverage of the body is perhaps the easiest to understand and is often what people are trying to say when they simply say "leverage." Jones calls it getting into a "position of power," where the player is not just lower than the other player, but the center of gravity is lower, muscles are engaged, and the player is able to apply the power. Being able to push someone around is nice, but if a defender rushes to the wrong point and leaves an open spot for a trap or cutback, that leverage is worthless.

Not only does this leveraged position of power need to be acted on within the context of the play, it has to be controlled. The defender usually has a slight advantage physically, but also doesn't know the intent of the offensive play call, which are usually designed to counteract a particular defensive look and intent. John Madden, the legendary coach and announcer, used to regularly say that big defensive linemen "took up a lot of space." Pure size aside, these 350-pound behemoths sometimes did just that, blocking up an area of the field with just their presence.

I spoke with Hugh Douglas, the former first round pick, All-Pro, and Super Bowl participant. Douglas was a 6'2, 280-pound defensive lineman who played most of his career with the Philadelphia Eagles. "You have to get your center of gravity below his," Douglas said. "Offensive linemen like to sit down with their back straight, like they're in a chair and get their base. If you can get under them and move that base, they can't use their power to steer you."

If an offensive play is designed to come through the center of the line and there's a big strong guy just standing there, whether or not he does anything is often irrelevant. He's disrupted the intent of the play, if not the execution. The late Howard Mudd, the longtime offensive line coach with the Indianapolis Colts, told me in 2012 that an offensive play design is only half of it. "It's half script, half improvisation," he said in an interview for *Sports Illustrated*. "Nothing goes as called. If the defense just clogs it up, makes the runner juke around, and gets two yards, the defense won."

Douglas concurred. "When I was with the Eagles, Jim Johnson [the legendary defensive coordinator] would install a certain defense and then my instincts would take over, so he'd adjust the defense to what I was doing. A good defensive coordinator plays to the strengths of his players. Guys like Ray Lewis or Brian Dawkins, both Hall of Famers for a reason, they had a lot of freedom in the defense."

That kind of leverage is key, fighting off not only blocks but directed motion. If a defensive edge rusher decides (or is instructed) to make a speed rush around the offensive line on a play where the ball is coming just inside the tackle, he's in the wrong place and not in position to plant and get back to the play. Similarly, a speed rush can often be met with leverage, pushing the defender just slightly further out, enough to run past the quarterback with arms flailing.

If you picture that giant nose tackle, you'll understand why he's partially the creation of the weight room and partially that of the training table, as well as a healthy dose of genetics. A player at 300 pounds is simply harder to move than one at 250. Teach him good technique and create a low center of gravity and a position where he can explode and move athletically, even at that size, and a football coach becomes a modern Frankenstein, creating monsters.

Then again, the biggest doesn't always win. This is where something like hand leverage comes in. The modern NFL is more permissive for offenses, part of protecting quarterbacks. Offensive linemen use their hands and even grab defenders, so there's a quick game of slap fight at the beginning of every play. The defender has to get leverage to get a blocker's hands either off him entirely or at least not at a point that the blocker can lock him up legally.

"Up and in" is how a current defensive line coach explained his technique to me. He teaches a basic technique where the defender explodes off the line with his center of gravity lower than the blocker's, but that his hands get inside position, like a wrestler or UFC fighter. "If the blocker has his hands in, he can extend and move [my guy]," he explained. "I want his hands out, then having to come back in. He's got to try and squeeze me like a grape and with his arms out, the referee is more likely to flag it" for a holding call.

Of course, the easy counter is to have the blocker's hands starting in, nearly centered. That's exactly opposite of where they want to be. "The blocker can do that, but I've already won," said the D-line coach again. "He needs his arms out, pushing, extending on me. A diamond push up is harder than a regular one and that's what he's doing if he does something simple and foolish like that. You'll never see it at this level."

That hand leverage takes another step as the defender makes a step. Again, focused on the defensive line here, where contact with the blocker is nearly instant, there's two major reactions. Either the blocker is coming forward for a run, or he's going backwards into pass protection. In both situations, the defender wants his hands as free as possible, unless they're being productively used against the blocker or blockers.

It's more complex than a simple equal-and-opposite. While a defender wants to not do what the blocker wants him to do, the same is true on the other side, but there's more options for the defender, even if some of those aren't the proper choice. The D-line coach detailed this for me. "My guy has to use his hands to get free and then keep his hands free to wrap up the tackle. Maybe it's a pass play and if I can't get to the quarterback, I can get my hands up and maybe deflect one. Maybe it's a run and I see the running back cutting, so I get free of the blocker and take him down." Those are all good, but with each of those choices, there's also more than a bit of a chance that a player will go the wrong way or move out of his area enough to create an opening for a modern mobile quarterback.

Hugh Douglas said that technique usually beats strength. "If a [blocker] is sound, if he can move with you like a mirror drill, that's always hard," he explained. "He can go with you inside and then you shift back outside and the good technique guy, he's with you. He's never overextended, he's never having to just bull you.

A strong guy is tough, but technique will usually win in the NFL. Everyone's strong, not everyone is sound."

The final leverage is the most brutal, that of attack leverage. This is most applicable to linebackers, just behind the play and often free of blockers on most plays. On a simple run, the linebacker will read the motion of the line versus where the scheme of the defense is anticipated. In many schemes, he's watching two gaps and is called on to quickly close any opening hole. That's done in almost all cases with attack leverage, which is simply closing hard and fast to where the runner will be.

This is where force equals mass times acceleration in the most basic sense. Like two rams fighting by butting heads, attack leverage is simply delivering force in the most brutal way possible. The big hits are when the physics of the issue don't match up, such as a runner slowed and hit by an offsides linebacker when he wasn't expecting it, or seeing a runner accelerate a few steps, only to be met by a closing safety's shoulder in his sternum.

The scariest part of this is when the forces are extremely mismatched or additive. We mostly see this on head-to-head (sometimes literally) and pure perpendicular hits, where the shift in force causes very noticeable vector changes. The NFL has tried to reduce these with rules to penalize hits on "defenseless receivers," blindside blocks, and with leading with the helmet on hits. However, the NFL can't legislate against physics, nor convince offensive coordinators that crossing routes don't work.

However, the most dangerous one is the hit where force is applied to a non-moving object. This is almost always a quarterback taking a hit from an edge rusher. There is so much force that several years ago, an NFL doctor told me that most defensive players lose an inch of height over the course of their football career, due to spinal compression from the force of the hits. However, quarterbacks get slightly taller, due to the spinal extension when they get hit from behind.

The final area of force leverage is the application through bodies. Yes, through. Think of this like bowling or pool, where the ball hits the top pin or ball and things cascade through the rack. Sometimes it's enough to hit someone and knock them into someone else. This is most often seen at the goal line, when defenses often just blindly charge gaps, guessing the play is most likely a sneak or power run. Stopping any push and knocking guys back is often very much like bowling with human pins.

Hugh Douglas explained that one of the hardest things he dealt with as an NFL player is when the ball carrier came at him while he was still engaged with a blocker. "The best way I can describe it is like a bucking bronco," he explained with a laugh. "There's no form tackle to it. You're just doing the best you can to shed the blocker, get him off you, and make a tackle or at least slow the runner down."

One thing that is almost unknown is the amount of force and/ or pressure for all of these. While it's calculable given existing data, there's been very few instances where pressure sensors or any sort of force gauge has been used, and none of those have been in major game situations. We can see the force and the players certainly feel it, but along with bigger/stronger/faster, we've also had harder or at the very least more. That's not going to change and could, in fact, be something that still grows linearly over the next quarter century of the game.

Coverage

Tampa 2. Cover 0. Nickel. Dime. Double.

Football is a sport of lingo and when it comes to defining how receivers are covered by the pairing of defensive backs (cornerbacks and safeties), plus linebackers and even linemen in some special situations, that lingo can get confusing. However, it all comes back to simple principles based on geometry and trigonometry.

A smash-mouth defense isn't where you'd expect higher level

math and if asked, few players if any could tell you the underlying principles. They don't have to and you don't want your safety over the top trying to calculate a vector when he's got Ja'Marr Chase trying to run under a Joe Burrow deep ball. You want the players to know the coverage so well they never have to think about the math.

Dennis Allen was named the new head coach of the New Orleans Saints after longtime coach Sean Payton decided to hang it up. Allen has been the defensive coordinator with the Saints since leaving his first head coaching job and his success in that role earned him a second try at the top job. One big reason for that is his success against Tom Brady's Buccaneers teams over the past few seasons.

Allen's defense is a 4-3 in name but since 2016, the team has actually lined up more in nickel packages with five defensive backs. In essence this is a 4-2-5, with three safeties.

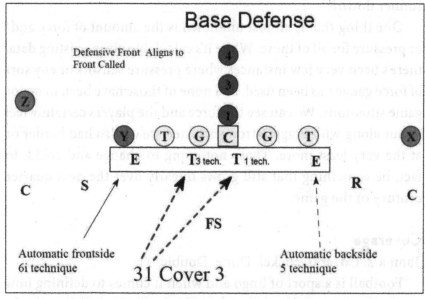

4-2-5 base defense. *Diagram courtesy of 425defense.com*

The Saints tend to use three safeties in the nickel versus three corners, with the change coming depending on personnel, down, and game situation. Against a team like the Bucs, heavy with tight ends Rob Gronkowski and Cameron Brate, the bigger safety should be a plus, while also helping more with the run game.

Using the nickel package (five defensive backs, usually taking out a linebacker) or similar variants has gone from uncommon to near-standard, with many teams joining the Saints in making it their most used defensive set. Alternating what that back five is also is becoming more common, but the Saints take it not one, but two steps further.

The first change is that Allen never seemed reluctant to give more coverage as necessary, using the dime package—six defensive backs and one linebacker—more than any other team the last two seasons, according to Pro Football Focus. This usually manifested itself with three safeties, including one over the tight end, or two in two-tight end sets.

Allen also gives multiple looks with his safeties, with two or three at the back—the "top"—to prevent deep throws. While the two or three safety looks are called Cover 2 or Cover 3 for obvious reasons, the way modern coordinators look at it are whether the middle of the field is closed—a safety there, between the hashes—or open, with that middle of the field beginning uncovered. The call "MOFO" from a quarterback ahead of the play indicates the middle of the field is open (MOFO is simply an acronym here) and can change routes from the called play.

Again, it's not that simple. A Cover 2 with the middle of the field open almost always carries a rotation, where the two safeties will shift to a side, leaving the corner on the non-shift side to drop back in man coverage. This can be a weakness if the quarterback can find it.

The switch between man and zone defenses along with multiple looks, and even some hybrid coverages (both man and zone by different defenders) makes this a much tougher read for the quarterback. These are becoming much more common, either against a key receiver, where a single defender is assigned to him as we often see against talents like Tyreek Hill or Ja'Marr Chase, or where the defense is trying to cause a misread by the quarterback.

These misreads are exacerbated by personnel that can do multiple things. A linebacker that can edge rush, blitz inside, or drop into coverage can't be read until he does one of those things in the play. Having one on each side makes it nearly impossible for any quarterback to read both properly. Adding more and more personnel that can do multiple things from any set makes it exponentially harder, which can lead to broken plays, indecision hesitation, or worse, a mistake.

What Allen has done with his 4-2-5 defense with the Saints is spreading around the league as the talent adjusts to the demands. Doing one thing well isn't enough when a base defense could call on a player to do one of many things on any given play.

Coverage is also being adjusted to the multi-functional or "positionless" defense. In 2018, Gary Patterson, then the head coach at Texas Christian, not only used a 4-2-5 hybrid to try and stymie Oklahoma's speedy Kyler Murray, he used players who weren't actually defenders simply to get enough speed on the field. Patterson used a backup quarterback as a standup edge linebacker and backup linebackers as both safeties and down linemen. The flexibility was nice and the scheme solid, but Murray and Oklahoma put up 52 points on the defense and won.

No matter how a defense gets into coverage, sets itself into a zone shape, or mans up against a key receiver, there's going to be both successes and failures. The continued evolutions we see are going in two directions, risk-averse and risk-acceptance. Many defenses like the basic Cover 2 or Cover 3 are being used to deny big plays. This is "bend don't break" at its finest. Sets like the 4-2-5 hybrid are much more willing to risk in order to create turnovers and break down an offense's tendencies, but will give up the (hopefully) occasional big play when there's a mistake, misread, or execution gap.

Deciding that philosophy is at the very center of the modern defense. How much risk are you willing to take, and how do you set up to counter an offensive tendency from play to play. Everything else is adjustable.

In Defense of the Modern Defense

To summarize, defense is more than just a cat and mouse game, a reaction to every offensive action. Instead, modern defenses use modern principles to create imbalances, force decisions, and disguise their placements.

Hugh Douglas made an interesting point during our talk. "So much of this is hard for fans to see. The call changes the assignment," he explained. "Sometimes I have inside gap, sometimes it's outside. If I'm supposed to be covering that gap and someone goes inside me, I didn't get beat. I still have to try and make a play, but it's not like I did nothing. Without knowing the play call and the intent, it's tougher to tell if someone got beat or if the coach got beat."

A simple thought experiment posed to me by an NFL defensive coordinator shows what a defense has to go through. "What if you knew every play? What if the quarterback came to the line and just called out what he was going to do? Could you stop it? How quickly could you react if you have the wrong call or the wrong personnel? If you could, is that play something that adjusts or reads? Could that offense simply out-execute the defense on any given play?"

The answer to all these questions is maybe. Even with the theoretical perfect call on both sides, there is still a talent and execution gap, one exacerbated by factors outside the control of the coaches and even the players, like fatigue or vision. The game remains unpredictable because defenses haven't been able to shut down all the vagaries, all the options, and close it to a mere execution equation. At least not yet.

SPECIAL TEAMS

Special teams are often ignored.

The worst teams in the NFL will still make more than 80 percent of their extra points and more than 60 percent of their field goals. Kickoffs are typically sandwiched by commercials, and the punt team coming out onto the field is typically a sign for fans watching at home or in person to squeeze in a bathroom break or grab a drink.

But how important is special teams, and how much actually goes into preparation for that phase in each week of practice? The old coaching adage is that "special teams are one-third of the game," but that doesn't always seem like it's the case.

For one team in particular, oversight on special teams will haunt them for the rest of their lives.

The 2010 San Diego Chargers are arguably the most dominant team in modern NFL history to miss the playoffs. Despite having the top-ranked offense and defense in terms of yardage, the Chargers went just 9–7, missing the postseason entirely.

On paper, the Chargers should have been a Super Bowl contender. The team featured four different Pro Bowl players that year, including quarterback Philip Rivers and future Hall of Fame tight end Antonio Gates. The defense boasted a premiere pass rusher in Shaun Phillips and a lockdown secondary that featured Eric Weddle, Antoine Cason, and Quentin Jammer.

So how did a team with 6,329 yards of offense and only 4.345 yards allowed on defense miss the playoffs entirely? A special teams unit that was historically bad.

The Chargers started that season going just 2–5, losing games due to a variety of special teams blunders. They allowed 160 punt return yards in a 21–14 loss to the Kansas City Chiefs in their season opener. Two weeks later, Seattle Seahawks running back Leon Washington tied an NFL record with two kickoff return touchdowns, handing the Chargers their second loss of the season.

Special teams continued to kill the Chargers as the season went on. A Week Five loss to the Oakland Raiders featured blocked punts on two consecutive drives, a feat so rare that SB Nation's *Secret Base* YouTube series calculated the odds of blocks happening on two straight punts at roughly 42,000 to 1.

San Diego fought back into playoff contention in the second half of the year, finishing 7–2 in their final nine games. Unfortunately for the Chargers, it wasn't enough to make the playoffs in a tightly-contested AFC.

Special teams weren't the only reason that the Chargers missed out on the playoffs, but they played a big factor. Their 18.9 yards allowed per punt return are the worst in NFL history since 1970, and their four blocked punts accounted for one-third of all punts blocked across the NFL during the 2010 season.

Despite the 2010 Chargers being a cautionary tale on the importance of special teams, coaches at all levels of the game continue to focus on offense and defense rather than pouring resources into that phase of the game. Perhaps it could be because the NFL, along with its competition committee, have contemplated phasing out certain parts of special teams entirely.

In March 2018, Green Bay Packers president Mark Murphy, a member of the league's competition committee, told reporters that the NFL would consider removing kickoffs altogether to make the game safer. He suggested a dramatic course of action could be on the table if data showed that kickoffs weren't becoming safer despite recent rule changes.

"If you don't make changes to make it safer, we're going to do away with it," Murphy warned. "It's that serious. It's by far the most dangerous play in the game."

Kickoff returns tend to feature the most violent collisions in the sport, simply because of the velocity at which players run at each other. The kickoff team takes off at a full sprint from the 40-yard line towards the ball carrier, typically 45 to 50 yards, while the return man catching the kickoff must run at full speed towards them.

The NFL has implemented changes to increase the number of touchbacks on kickoff returns. When a player catches the ball in the end zone and takes a knee, or the ball bounces into the end zone, the receiving team will automatically get the ball at their own 25-yard line.

In 2016, the NFL changed their touchback rules to give the receiving team the ball at the 25-yard line instead of the 20. In 2011, the NFL moved the kickoff from the 35-yard line to the 40. These two rule changes helped lead to a record number of touchbacks in 2020, with kickoffs resulting in a touchback 61.2 percent of the time.

Despite the increased number of touchbacks, injuries still occur on the play. In Week Eight of the 2021 season, Green Bay Packers return man Kylin Hill and Arizona Cardinals running back Jonathan Ward collided on a kickoff taken out of the end zone. Both players were carted off the field, with Hill suffering a season-ending knee injury.

It's uncertain what the NFL will do to reduce the number of injuries on kickoffs, or if they will get rid of the play altogether. However, former Stanford center Sam Schwartzstein believes he has the answer to fixing the league's kickoff problem.

Schwartzstein was born in Greenwich, Connecticut. When he was seven years old, he moved to Texas, where he was ultimately pulled into the sport because that's what everyone did in his hometown. His brother decided to start training him in sixth grade to help him eventually earn a college scholarship.

That training paid off, with Schwartzstein earning a scholarship to play at Stanford University. He was a center for the Cardinal, playing with the program for five years. He started all 13 games in 2011, snapping the ball to future number-one pick Andrew Luck.

Prior to the 2012 season, Schwartzstein was named a team

captain, helping lead Stanford to their first Rose Bowl victory since January 1972. He takes extreme pride in that accomplishment, joking that former teammates Luck and NFL All-Pro guard David DeCastro couldn't win a Rose Bowl during their college careers.

After college, Schwartzstein spent five years away from football in Silicon Valley working in product management. It wasn't until Oliver Luck, Andrew's father, reached out that Sam found another opportunity to get back into the game.

Oliver Luck was named the commissioner and CEO of the XFL in June 2018. The football league that had operated as a joint venture in 2001 with the WWE was planning on making a comeback thanks to WWE CEO Vince McMahon.

Working closely with the founder of the XFL's rebirth in McMahon, Luck quickly learned that the WWE chairman was looking to change the rules of the game, focusing on making the league's rules entertaining for fans without straying too far from the rules that football fans were accustomed to.

Luck hired Schwartzstein to become the XFL's director of football operations, innovation and strategy in July 2018. Sam was hired to help on multiple decisions including player compensation, designing the league's football, and most importantly, creating the new rules for the league.

"As we built out the rule change process, we knew that special teams was one of the big things that we wanted to change," Schwartzstein said.

Before creating the new rules, the XFL interviewed more than six thousand fans to get an idea of what they wanted to see changed in the game of football. The answers they received from those fans helped create what Sam called the four pillars that they used to create their rulebook. Those pillars were:

- Minimizing idle time to speed up the game
- Reducing meaningless plays

- Creating a more dynamic and rhythmic game
- Making the game safer without losing the feeling of traditional football

When the XFL signed a broadcasting deal with ESPN and FOX, McMahon was focused on several things to make the game more appealing. That included the elimination of kickoffs being sandwiched by commercial breaks, speeding up instant replay reviews, and reducing the number of penalties without sacrificing player safety.

Some of those big changes required new rules to keep the game flowing. Schwartzstein said that he went line by line through the NFL rulebook and asked "why?" on every single rule. Most NFL rules are intended for player safety, but other rules such as having specific jersey numbers tied to certain positions and responsibilities felt a bit more arbitrary.

For any potential rule changes, Schwartzstein and the league wanted to make sure that they fit into one of their four pillars. If a rule didn't fit within one of the pillars, the league leaned towards maintaining tradition in order to avoid making the product feel gimmicky. That was where special teams became a huge focus for Schwartzstein and his team.

"Fans don't hate special teams," Schwartzstein said. "They just want it to be exciting."

The main pillar that their new special teams rules focused on was reducing meaningless plays. Schwartzstein wanted to reduce the number of plays that involved almost no action, specifically kickoffs for touchbacks, kicks and punts going out of bounds, and fair catches. More than 60 percent of punts and kickoffs in the NFL were deemed meaningless plays according to Schwartzstein's research.

The XFL wanted to find a means to keep the game traditional and safe while finding ways to give fans more action on special teams. That was especially true for kickoffs, a play that results in a touchback and an untimed play more often that an actual return in the NFL.

According to Schwartzstein, 18 percent of injuries in the NFL occur on kickoffs, despite them only counting for 6 percent of all plays. Seeing that players were three times more likely to get hurt on kickoffs, he wanted to see what specifically caused the injuries to occur.

The problem was that players on the kicking team were traveling more than 35 yards to make contact with blockers and the ballcarrier on kicks that were returned. That kind of momentum created high-collision impacts that led to more injured players.

The XFL's solution was simple, yet effective. Instead of having the kicking team's players start where the kickoff happened, the league instead moved every single player besides the kicker and the return man within five yards of each other before the kick. The kicking team would start on the 35-yard line, while the receiving team started on the 30-yard line. Once the ball was kicked, all players besides the return man and kicker would have to wait until the ball was fielded by the return man to begin the play.

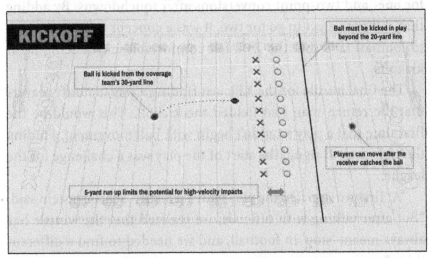

XFL kickoff rule graphic. *Image courtesy Sam Schwartzenstein*

The major issue Schwartzstein saw with this new rule and their four pillars was that it would effectively remove the surprise onside kick, one of the more exciting plays in the game. Before scrapping the new kickoff rule, Schwartzstein wanted to see how often surprise onside kicks happened.

"You look at onside kicks and they're 1 percent of all kicks," Schwartzstein said. "All surprise onside kicks are only 1 percent of those. So for a basis point of all kicks, we would be keeping concussions in the game. The only time one basis point matters is when you're dealing with large investment funds."

Ultimately, Schwartzstein and his team decided to move forward with their proposed kickoff rules, allowing kickoff teams to move their players back towards the kicker only by electing to attempt an onside kick by notifying officials.

Fortunately for the XFL, the NFL had already done something similar with elections and extra points. After moving extra-point attempts back from the two-yard line to the 15-yard line, the NFL introduced the ability for teams to elect to go for two at the spot closer to the end zone. This created completely different rules for one- and two-point conversions after touchdowns. By adding that ability to elect to go for two, it was a concept familiar enough to football fans that the XFL felt comfortable introducing it for kickoffs.

The final hurdle for the XFL was finding a way to notify players that the return man had fielded the kickoff. This would be the first time that a play wouldn't begin with ball movement. Finding the right way to signal the start of the play was a challenge for the league.

"At first we signaled the play with a whistle," Schwartzstein said. "But after talking with officials, we realized that the whistle has always meant 'stop' in football, and we needed to find a different thing."

The XFL workshopped different ways to signal the start of play, testing out the use of a foghorn, a flag, and eventually ended up having an official raising their arm before play and lowering it once the play was able to begin.

Once the rules for kickoffs were drawn up, Schwartzstein needed to pitch it to coaches, players, and health professionals. The emphasis on the latter was making sure that the new rules would reduce the number of concussions and injuries on kickoffs, rather than increase them by having the players all closer together before the play began.

After pitching the rules, the XFL needed to test them and see if they worked on the field. Schwartzstein and his team tested the rules across the country, from Mississippi junior colleges to an interactive football league known as Your Call Football. By holding tests in different environments, the XFL was able to collect enough data to see if their rules were viable.

Schwartzstein believes that what made his rules for the XFL work so well was something known as "invisible efficiency." The concept is that the rules work effectively enough that the more intricate details of them are rarely shown to the average football fan, simply because the rules incentivize the game to be played in a certain way.

An example Schwartzstein uses to demonstrate invisible efficiency was a play made by Green Bay Packers return man Ty Montgomery in 2016. During a game against the Detroit Lions, a kickoff was bouncing near the sideline. Rather than fielding the ball as he normally would, Montgomery intentionally went out of bounds, then laid down prone into the field of play to grab the ball. It's not a rule the casual football fan would know, but Montgomery's heads-up play resulted in a penalty for a kickoff going out of bounds, resulting in Green Bay getting to start their offensive drive on the 40-yard line.

Montgomery was incentivized to make a heads-up play to give his team better field position. Using the ideas of invisible efficiency and incentive-based rule design, Schwartzstein found a way to reduce meaningless plays and create more return opportunities.

In order to keep kickers from kicking out of the end zone or out of bounds, the XFL opted for harsher starting field position for the returning team. Rather than starting at the 25-yard line after a touchback in the NFL, the return team would start at the 35-yard line in the XFL. A kickoff out of bounds would be played another 20 yards downfield at the kicking team's 45-yard line.

The rules made it much more punitive for teams wanting to avoid kickoff returns, resulting in significantly fewer touchbacks and kicks out of bounds. Going along with invisible efficiency, fans would be far less likely to know about the rule because the kickers would be incentivized to avoid those kinds of plays at all costs.

In fact, the rules for kickoffs naturally created a consistent target zone for the kickers to aim for, in front of the end zone and between the hashes. It made fielding kickoffs much easier for a single return man who wasn't as concerned about where the ball was going, knowing that the kickers were trying to avoid touchbacks and out of bounds penalties. These incentive-based rules resulted in a staggering 93 percent of kickoffs being returned.

The kickoff rules also helped with the XFL's goal of more points being scored in their games. One of the easiest ways to help teams score more points is by having them start closer to the opponent's end zone, which was something the kickoff rules were aiming to do. At the same time, however, the XFL didn't want every single kickoff being returned for a touchdown.

"Everyone had opinions about our rules," Schwartzstein said. "So many people were saying 'this is going to be a touchdown every time' or 'the defense is going to win every time.' It was brand new, and we needed to test it out."

The data for the XFL's kickoff rules were promising. The average starting field position for teams was the 31-yard line compared to the 28-yard line in the NFL, and two of the league's kickoffs were returned for touchdowns.

Most importantly, the XFL had *zero* injuries on their kickoffs throughout the league's entire existence.

Despite their success, Schwartzstein is the first to admit that his rules weren't perfect. When testing his rules at The Spring League, the first kickoff that occurred resulted in the kick hitting the ground, and the return man walking up to the ball and acting as if the play had been blown dead. Once the ball hit the field, Schwartzstein realized that he had never accounted for what would happen if the ball wasn't fielded and hit the field of play.

"You can't account for stupidity," Schwartzstein said. "Not every play that happens or every player is going to act logically."

The XFL ended up adding a rule to account for the ball hitting the field of play, allowing the return man three seconds to pick up the ball before it was blown dead.

Schwartzstein also acknowledged that the more skilled kickers in the XFL were able to take advantage of some of his rules. Kickers who could place the ball well and drive it low enough to bounce it into the field of play before hitting the end zone could influence the receiving team into taking a "minor" touchback. In the XFL's kickoff rules, a minor touchback resulted in the ball being placed at only the 15-yard line after the ball bounced from the field of play into the end zone, was recovered by the return man, and then kneeled to blow the play dead.

"Not every rule was perfect," Schwartzstein said. "We did have some holes in the rules. But we eliminated high collisions [on kickoffs] and ended up with zero injuries."

Schwartzstein deservedly takes great pride in the XFL's reduction in injuries. He acknowledges that there was one occurrence of a player injuring his ankle on a kickoff, but that he did end up continuing to play through the game.

"A part of me wishes there were more injuries," Schwartzstein said.

"Because that would at least make the stat seem less ridiculous. You're not going to have four hundred plays in football and have zero injuries, so how did we have around four hundred kickoffs without any?"

Getting coaches on board with the new rules wasn't always easy, Schwartzstein admitted. Some teams tried to have their blockers sprint back to the return man to create a wedge to lead the way for the return man. However, the XFL implemented a rule to prevent return teams from having their blockers retreat to avoid high-speed collisions that caused most kickoff injuries in the NFL.

Coaches quickly got on board once they saw the rules play out on the field, and the kickoffs quickly caught the eye of a national audience. Considering the XFL's data on injuries and the popularity of the league's rule change, Schwartzstein believes that the NFL should strongly consider adopting his changes to kickoffs rather than getting rid of them entirely.

"I think my rule is the future of kickoff," Schwartzstein said. "The league may lose the surprise onside kick, but they'd be greatly reducing injuries while also increasing the number of returns and opportunities for 100-yard touchdowns that we rarely get to see in the NFL anymore."

Schwartzstein reiterated the importance of keeping kickoffs in football, stressing their cultural impact on the game. The beginning of the Super Bowl would be a lot less ceremonious if a team automatically started on the 25-yard line rather than having a team kick the ball away. The play even has a place in our lexicon, with people starting projects or meetings by "kicking things off."

"I know it sounds like me smelling my own farts, but I feel that football does have a piece of culture in America that is important," Schwartzstein said. "And I do believe that kickoffs are part of that culture."

The NFL may very well get rid of kickoffs in the not-too-distant future. Their internal rule changes have focused more on turning the kickoff into a meaningless play rather than reducing injuries while keeping the excitement of the return. There is some hope for the revival of kickoffs, however. In February 2022 the NFL announced a partnership with the XFL to collaborate on health, safety, and technology innovations.

It's unclear at the time of writing if this partnership will review changes in kickoff rules. However, according to Schwartzstein, implementing his rules from the XFL would be the best way for the league to keep the kickoff alive while keeping its players safe.

Kicking the Kickers

Certain aspects of special teams tend to be overlooked by the average fan, but most fans easily understand the amount of pressure that goes into a kicker trying to make a field goal in high-stress situations.

Kickers represent the top 25 highest-scoring players in NFL history, with the position requiring them to kick extra points after every touchdown and field goals when their team is unable to cap off a drive in the end zone. Adam Vinatieri leads the NFL with 2,673 points in a career that lasted more than two decades.

Even the average kicker in the NFL is consistently putting up points, to the point where fans will assume the vast majority of field goals and extra points will be successful. According to ESPN, the success rate for field goals in the NFL between 2015 and 2020 was at 83.6 percent. For extra points, even with the rule changes bringing the attempt back to the 15-yard line, the success rate has hovered around 94 percent.

Extra points rarely have a major impact on the outcome of a game, but a missed field goal at the end of a contest can have backbreaking consequences for a team, both in the game and for the rest of the season.

The mental component of kicking gets put under a microscope because of these clutch situations. Where other positions in football must read and react instantaneously to what is going on around them, kickers have time to set up and think before executing. In high-pressure situations like game-winning field-goal attempts, this can lead to overthinking, anxiety, and miscues in execution.

Football coaches are aware of the mental burden placed on kickers in these high-pressure situations, which is why "icing the kicker" continues to be a common strategy for teams.

Icing the kicker is a term for calling a timeout immediately before a kicker attempts a field goal. The strategy is used to throw off a kicker's timing and give them more time to think about their kick.

Data has shown that icing the kicker has been an effective strategy in high-pressure situations in recent years. In a 2021 study from Sports Info Solutions, Nathan Cooper tracked kicks throughout the NFL to see the difference in success rates from kickers when they were iced versus not iced, specifically in the final three minutes of each half and overtime.

From 2015 through 2018, Cooper found that kickers who were not iced made 80.9 percent of their field-goal attempts in these clutch situations. When a timeout was called before their attempt, however, that success rate dropped down to just 68.1 percent.

One infamous example of icing the kicker working out was the "Double Doink."

In January 2019, the Philadelphia Eagles faced the Chicago Bears in a low-scoring NFC wild-card game. After a late go-ahead touchdown by Nick Foles and the Eagles, the Bears had just a minute left to get into field-goal range to try and win the game.

Mitch Trubisky was able to lead the Bears down the field thanks to a pair of crucial passes before spiking the ball with just ten seconds left. The drive set up Cody Parkey for a makeable 43-yard field goal to win the game and send Chicago to the divisional round.

Before Parkey's first attempt, Eagles head coach Doug Pederson called a timeout to ice Parkey, who sent a practice field-goal attempt through the uprights. The second attempt didn't go nearly as well after the timeout, with Parkey's attempt ricocheting off the left upright, bouncing off the crossbar, then falling onto the field. The sound of the ball coming off the posts—a literal double doink—still haunts Bears fans.

The Bears lost the game 16–15, and Parkey never kicked another field goal or extra point for Chicago. He was released by the team on March 13, just two months after missing the game-winning field goal.

Psychology can have a huge impact on athletes, but kickers are in a different category given the way that they operate. According to Adam Shunk, the position requires exceptional mental toughness.

Adam is a professional sports psychologist for the Indiana Pacers and Butler University in Indianapolis. Before he was a psychologist, he was a decorated track and field athlete, competing in the high jump in the 2006 World Indoor Championships and 2007 Pan American Games.

Initially trying to help himself as an athlete, Adam graduated with a bachelor's degree in psychology from the University of North Carolina before getting his master's degree and PhD from Ball State University in the same field.

After he suspected his track career was ending, Adam wanted to continue to be involved in high-level athletics. He then decided to attain all the graduate coursework and licensure requirements to become a sports psychologist and has been practicing for the past 15 years.

Over his decade and a half as a sports psychologist, Adam has worked with several Division I football programs, along with several professional placekickers and punters. After working with them firsthand, he has a strong handle on what it takes to be successful at the position.

"There are so many athletes that can kick a football accurately, but doing it consistently under pressure is truly a unique skillset," Adam said. "On a continuum of sports, I think a kicker is right up there with golf as having the highest amount of mental demands compared to raw physical abilities."

Although college and NFL kickers tend to have great leg strength, they typically don't have to be in top-tier physical shape due to the low-impact nature of the position.

The mental component is different for kickers compared to other football players. The comparisons from kickers to golfers makes more sense psychologically, since both are preparing for their kicks/shots rather than quickly reacting to what develops in front of them like other players.

"Most great kickers have a very regimented mental routine that they do before every single kick," Adam said. "This often requires some behavioral sequence to get ready and physically prepared, relaxation techniques such as deep breathing to bring their energy down, and a cue word or focus strategy to stay focused on what they have control of and prevent distractions in their environment."

Because of this routine, icing the kicker seems to have a tangible impact on reducing the accuracy of kickers in clutch situation, at least according to recent data from Sports Info Solutions.

"When you ice a kicker they have to restart their preparation process," Adam said. "It creates an opportunity to break rhythm and distraction to manage. They have to restart the process and sometimes the time to think, a distraction or break in their rhythm could potentially throw them off."

Even with the data provided, Shunk likes to think that the NFL's best kickers aren't fazed by opposing teams calling timeouts in big moments. He believes that the league's best have mentally rehearsed situations where their rhythm might be thrown off, and that their structured mental routine can be easily restarted in order to refocus and avoid any loss in accuracy.

A missed potential game-winning field goal can be devastating for the average fan, but considering the mental fortitude it takes to succeed as an NFL kicker, it's a testament to the league's best at how dependable they can be in these high-pressure situations.

Even if fans mostly ignore special teams, the importance of them can't be overstated. The Green Bay Packers know that all too well from the horrific ending to their 2021 season.

The Packers had the NFL's best record in the 2021 regular season, earning a first-round bye before playing the San Francisco 49ers in the NFC divisional round. Special teams had been a huge problem for the Packers all season, but they had been able to get through their first 17 games without disastrous consequences.

Those consequences were felt by the entire Packers fan base in that playoff game. With the Packers up seven with less than five minutes remaining and punting out of their own end zone, poor execution resulted in Corey Bojorquez's punt being blocked and recovered for a game-tying touchdown.

The 49ers went on to advance thanks to a game-winning field goal as time expired. The Packers only had ten players on the field as they tried to block the attempt.

The 2010 Chargers and 2021 Packers serve as reminders for teams wanting to deprioritize special teams. It may not be the most exciting part of the game, but a limited special teams unit can destroy even the most dominant teams.

INJURIES

The very game of football has always been beset by injuries, even defined by it. From the early days where the deaths of the Ivy League students brought about a Teddy Roosevelt-led summit to today's congressional hearings on concussions and painkillers, the existential threat to the game's growth and even survival has been the brutality of the game itself and the injuries it inflicts on its players, short- and long-term.

I'm not here to judge the game for this, or even to relitigate the type of bad faith dealings that the NFL had with the concussion issue in recent years. Instead, the love of the game and medical science have come together outside the walls of the game and created ways for the game to survive and thrive, often in spite of the NFL rather than because of it.

There is an unholy trinity of injuries in football—head, spine, and knee injuries truly define the game across the century-plus of popularity. How football has dealt with these has largely been to ignore them, but the game seems to be surrounded by better angels, finding just enough of a fix to get past any public outcry at the same time that it actually makes the game better.

The best example of this is Joe Namath and his knee. The brash Jets quarterback was one of the first modern superstars of the game, his personality more Hollywood than western Pennsylvania, but he became a hero in Tuscaloosa, Alabama, playing for the storied Crimson Tide and Bear Bryant. It's an unlikely pairing, but one that almost didn't happen due to a severe knee injury. Namath had surgery and went on to win in college and then again in the pros, but his knee was never the same, affecting his game after just a few years, and ending his career early.

The surprising thing to most is that Namath's injury actually wasn't serious, or wouldn't be in a modern context. Namath didn't tear ligaments or tendons. Instead, it was a torn meniscus that was removed, a procedure called a meniscectomy. When done in the early 1960s, it was a big deal, involving a full leg brace and a major rehabilitation plan. Today, that same surgery would keep him out about two weeks, maybe a bit longer. NFL players have had the surgery the day after a game during the bye week and come back to play, no games missed.

The advances in knee surgery and the ability for players not just to come back, but to come back at the same level, is one of the biggest changes in the game. An anterior cruciate ligament (ACL) sprain is one of the most common injuries in football. If it happened in the 1960s or 1970s, it was a career ender for even the best in the NFL. Gale Sayers is considered one of the most physically gifted running backs to ever play the game, but his career was limited to just a handful of years after tearing his ACL in a 1968 game. He returned and was Comeback Player of the Year, but his knee was never the same. Instead, Sayers might be better remembered today for the movie that shows his rehab from that injury, done alongside his replacement, in the classic *Brian's Song*.

By the 1990s, ACL reconstruction was no longer a career ender, but it did alter careers. Billy Sims was the first overall pick and a prototype running back with speed, power, and what Barry Switzer, his college coach at Oklahoma, called "missability." Sims was one of the top backs from the moment he stepped foot in the NFL, but it quickly ended with a 1984 ACL injury. He attempted to come back not just for a couple seasons, but even tried again four years after the injury and extensive rehab. Sims today runs a chain of BBQ restaurants in Oklahoma and Missouri, but he declined to speak about his knee or his career when contacted.

By the 2000s, the technique had been perfected and surgeons like Dr. James Andrews, Dr. Neal ElAttrache, and a handful of super-surgeons around sports had made the ACL reconstruction something that was predictable. The injury happened and the player missed a year, but came back well. Over and over, players like Tom Brady, Saquon Barkley, Reggie Wayne, and hundreds of others did their time and were able to come back. In Brady's case, he's played as long after his ACL reconstruction as he did before, echoing Tommy John's career in baseball after his namesake surgery.

The surgery itself hadn't changed much, but the technique was honed. Autografts became the norm, using either a hamstring tendon from the injured athlete, or a section of patellar tendon, especially after the case of Carson Palmer. The Bengals quarterback had an allograft—one taken from another person, in his case an Achilles tendon from a young woman killed in a car wreck. Palmer later damaged the knee again and had a revision with an autograft.

Today, the procedure has been steady for more than two decades without much change, but plenty of practice for the doctors that Andrews and ElAttrache have trained. There are some changes, with support systems like InternalBrace and bridge-enhanced ACL repair (BEAR). These two surgeries use engineered systems made of high-tech materials like Kevlar to support the ligament, making the area stronger earlier and allowing for a more aggressive rehab, reducing time to return.

We're also seeing significant changes in how biologic agents are used. The use of platelet-rich plasma, aspirated stem cells, and more engineered solutions has grown in acceptance while results have been mixed.

When Jameson Williams went down, grabbing his knee near the logo of the 2022 College Football Playoff National Championship Game in Indianapolis, the certain first-rounder could have seen millions of dollars fade away. Because ACL surgery is so successful, Williams barely dropped in the NFL draft, going to the Detroit Lions at pick number 12. The Lions traded up twenty spots to get him, giving up picks because they felt Williams's injury didn't affect his future value. In the end, it barely cost Williams anything, even though he may not be ready to play at the start of his rookie year. It's a long way from the predictions that he would fall to the thirties pick, which would have cost him nearly $10 million dollars.

While an ACL (anterior cruciate ligament) sprain and reconstruction is less common in baseball than in football, the surgery is largely the same for any sport and has been for decades. There's significant evidence that Mickey Mantle had ACL surgery in the early 1950s, making him perhaps the earliest elite athlete to have the surgery. The surgery was first performed during World War II, though there are scant records.

(Note: Jane Leavy's excellent biography of Mantle comes to the opposite conclusion. Her thesis is that Mantle did *not* have his ACL reconstructed in 1953 and played the rest of his career without one.)

Williams had no such worries. He had barely hit the turf before tweets were fired out that he'd torn his ACL and would need surgery. There was no debate about what would be done or that there would be effects on his career in the long term. The surgery has come that far in the last seventy years and farther in the last twenty.

While there have been modifications to the surgery over the years, most have been evolutionary rather than revolutionary. The damaged ligament is removed and tunnels are drilled where a transplanted tendon, usually from a center-cut of the patient's own patellar tendon, is then looped through the holes and anchored in place.

It's relatively simple as a procedure and largely successful. There are variants on how and where the tunnels are placed, which tendon is used to reconstruct the damaged ligament, and there's some use of allografts, a donated tendon from another person, usually a cadaver's Achilles for size and strength.

This standard procedure has a common rehab as well and again, this has been more or less in place since the 1980s with only evolutionary changes. The biggest change has been a quicker weight-bearing phase, rather than waiting for the anchors to fully heal, which can take six to eight weeks.

It's not just elite athletes who suffer though, and certainly not just football players. ACL injuries are prominent at lower levels of football and rampant in female sports like soccer, volleyball, and basketball. All include a painful injury, an expensive surgery, and a long rehab with lost time, potentially ending a career or missing that final season of school-age competition.

ACL injuries can happen anywhere, even rural Chesapeake, West Virginia. Sports are big in the Mountain State, from perennial power West Virginia University to Marshall, a well-known Division I school, and huge in high school sports as well. It's this state, these valleys, the twisting roads from place to place, where Dr. Chad Lavender practices and where a new technique might completely change how ACL reconstruction is done and how athletes return from it.

Lavender's story is common to many orthopedic surgeons. He was an athlete himself, a long snapper at WVU, who realized his sports career was going no further. Lavender stayed at WVU for medical school and came to Marshall for his residency, where he's built an innovative practice.

"The key to all this is the support I get," said Dr. Lavender in a talk we had in January 2022. "Marshall Orthopedics and this community has allowed me to do so much. This is where I'm from, so I don't think I could have done this kind of thing at a Harvard, at a Stanford."

What Lavender has done is a modification of the surgery itself, again more of an evolution than revolution, but that has taken the return time from this kind of surgery and cut it by half and potentially more.

The surgery is called "Lavender Fertilized ACL" (I'll call it LFA for ease) and the description is dead on. The surgery itself is done arthroscopically—an "all inside" technique that is common but not ubiquitous in a world where open (large incision) surgery is still commonly done for this procedure. Dr. Lavender also uses an autograft that isn't common, using the quadriceps tendon rather than the patellar or hamstring tendon.

"It's a strong tendon for the graft," Lavender explained, "and anecdotally, people just seem to recover faster, so that's what I've focused on."

Lavender then supports the transplanted tendon with a piece of Arthrex SutureTape, a new procedure called InternalBrace. This is becoming more common in all sorts of joint reconstructions, with much of the focus on ankles and elbows. Lavender's use of the InternalBrace procedure helps guard the healing ligament and makes the overall construct stronger.

It's the next part where Lavender's procedure is radically different. For years, doctors have used biologic agents to help strengthen or heal areas. Common examples include platelet-rich plasma therapy, where the patient's blood is drawn, spun down to get to a more concentrated mixture, and injected back into the injured site, and more complex things like Orthokine. Lavender uses aspirated stem cells, or as Dr. Lavender says, stromal cells.

"We use a special demineralized bone matrix. You can work with it and put it up in those tunnels, in both the femur and the tibia," Lavender explained. "It has some staying power. Then a couple years ago, I realized that while I was drilling those tunnels, I could use that bone, the [patient's own] bone, and mix it in with the demineralized bone matrix." The bone shaving, which was normally discarded, is instead spun in a small centrifuge to get the stromal cells at a higher concentration. The bone shaving is then mixed with the stem cells and demineralized bone matrix into a putty, then used to fill the tunnels once the tendon is anchored into place.

Biologic agents like Lavender's "putty" are common and legal. Standard SutureTape comes with a collagen solution on the surface,

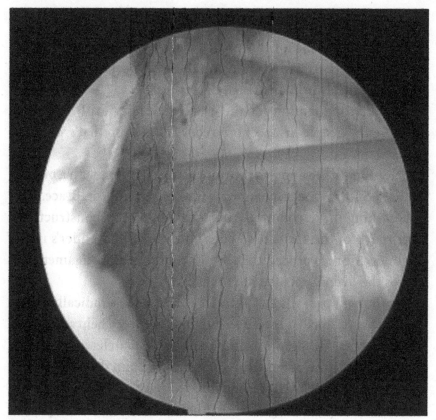

Dr. Lavender inserts his fertilized putty into a knee. *Photo courtesy Dr. Lavender*

but studies on its use show very little change in terms of efficacy. "It's like what you do with a potted plant," Lavender says. "That's why I call it a fertilized ACL. We're fertilizing that socket, waiting for the seeds to grow."

The combination of all these techniques makes up the complete procedure and they all contribute to the results. It's those results that really stand out.

In the most basic sense, the LFA procedure allows for the possibility of quicker healing, protects the graft more, and allows for a return to work or play in about half the time as the current standard procedure and rehab, though Dr. Lavender is careful never to emphasize that.

The rehab itself is not significantly different than that from normal ACL injuries, and have been handled by many physical therapists. "I get calls from them. The therapists continued to call me patient after patient, asking 'How am I supposed to react with patient X? He's already at the twelve-week timeframe, he's running at six weeks, what do you want me to do? Do you want me to hold him back?'", Lavender said. "I started to be very free with our PT protocol and basically started allowing them to return at their tolerance. I really didn't give them a lot of limitations other than no pivoting or cutting sports.

Lavender continued, "[The patients] routinely would would run at six to eight weeks, they routinely at twelve weeks would pass their testing to return to play! Still today, I hold athletes until the whole six-month period. I don't let them return to full activity, except for very isolated scenarios, where the benefit outweighed the risk for them to return early. That's where we are now. The research that I have shows at twelve weeks the operative knees are performing at 80 percent of the non-operative knees, which may correlate with earlier return to play at, say, four and a half months."

While Lavender holds to the six-month limit for return to sport, I had to ask about those limited situations. My guess was that he would be a bit freer for someone in their senior season. "You're exactly right," he said. "Basically, the timing has to work out to be four and a half months. It has to be a low-risk position, or someone that their livelihood depends on it, or a scholarship depends on it. Very few instances. The misconception is that we're out here returning kids to play at six weeks and that's not true. They are running and doing things [in therapy] at that point, but we haven't returned somebody that early, nor do we expect it. Now the four-and-a-half-month mark, I think is reasonable in the future based on the data."

Lavender isn't keeping his procedure a secret either. He's been teaching doctors around the country and some are doing the procedure themselves, though he's yet to see large numbers of doctors adopting the procedure. Overall, Lavender thinks the procedure has been done more than five hundred times, between himself, other surgeons at Marshall, and other doctors who have learned the technique.

Lavender explains that he doesn't think there's a problem with any other techniques. "I've always tried to make a point that this is more about research than it is to sit here and say, well, we've found the holy grail of ACL surgery," he says. "What we're saying is we're continuing to research this and we're really pleased with our early term results. We have a randomized trial that we've already finished enrollment in and some of that data is already finalized. We're really excited about the future of this technique."

Lavender continues, saying, "I think it's all how you frame things. You would never hear me say this is the only way to do it. That's not what I say. When I go out and talk to surgeons, I'm not telling them to stop doing patellar tendons or stop doing hamstrings. They should use what they think is best."

While Dr. Lavender does defer some to other approaches, that doesn't mean that he lacks confidence in what he's doing. "I feel like in five to ten years, every surgery will have some type of orthobiologic medium, following after what we're doing and kind of showing that thought process. It may not be my actual consistency, right or the composite graft that I use, but I think they'll have InternalBraces and I think there'll be some aspect of biology in those high-level athletes. I really believe that."

The easy thing to do to promote this surgery would be chase a big-name athlete. They've called, Lavender told me, but elite athletes seldom want to be first, especially with a change from a successful, predictable procedure. Teams have enquired too, but Lavender hasn't sought out a big name to promote his procedure.

"For example, a new study that came out a couple months ago, specifically looking at young female soccer players," Dr. Lavender explained. "They have about a 30 to 40 percent chance of another ACL injury under the age of 20. When you're faced with those type of issues and we talked about the return to play rates as low as 60 percent, that's what's given me so much passion towards the knee, the ACL, because there's so much we can improve on right. Standard rotator cuff, 90 to 95 percent of those patients do very well. That's one of the reasons that I focus so much on the ACL and on young athletes in West Virginia. That's my passion."

The other problem is that even cutting the return time in half isn't the cure-all for the ACL that many would hope for. Ronald Acuña Jr. had his knee injury on July 9, 2021 and had the surgery about a week later. Even at the most aggressive, had he not had the surgery, Acuña could not have come back from his injury in time to play in the World Series three months later. He would, however, have had a much shorter rehab time, allowing him to be more ready for the 2022 season.

We saw another example of why LFA could be game-changing with Saquon Barkley in 2021. Barkley, the star running back for the New York Giants, sprained his knee in the first week of the 2020 NFL season. He missed the rest of the season, but wasn't back to 100 percent by the start of the next season, a full year after his injury and subsequent surgery.

Barkley had the best of care and rehab, yet still struggled to come back. His 2021 season was a disappointment, and many pointed to a recent study done by Dr. Tim Hewett, a professor and researcher at the Mayo Clinic. Hewett's study is summarized in this quote from the paper, originally published in the *Journal of Sports Medicine*:

"[W]e present evidence in the literature that athletes achieve baseline joint health and function approximately 2 years after ACLR. We postulate that delay in returning to sports for nearly 2 years will significantly reduce the incidence of second ACL injuries."

However, even Hewett seems intrigued by the LFA. "I spoke

with Dr. Lavender at length at [a convention] and the technique sounds potentially promising," Hewett wrote in an email. "I'd say 'proceed with caution' given the biological considerations and cautions in our two-year paper."

Dr. Lavender agrees. "Dr. Hewett is absolutely correct and his research clearly shows there is evidence that if we wait longer we will have fewer re-ruptures," he said after hearing Dr. Hewett's quote. "However, the question is where is the risk/benefit ratio balance for return to play appropriate and also it is important to continue to study different novel techniques and subgroups that could return safely at earlier timepoints. Many surgeons certainly feel biologics and the InternalBrace could be the answer to that, but further study will be needed."

There's a question about whether people will need an accelerated return, whether for competitive or lifestyle reasons. If this surgery continues to prove effective, it will give people the option, something that doesn't exist today and could be extremely valuable. Everyone seems to agree with that, at least.

While most people focus on return to play, whether for elite or youth athletes, usually measured as a function of time, Dr. Lavender points to a more technical test as a better judge of why LFA is a better technique for many. That's what's simply called the hop test and it is a standard technique for measuring progress after any knee injury, requiring each patient to perform several types of single leg hops.

With a recent blind study, a group of patients were divided into two groups and tested by physical therapists that didn't know which group was which and tested them at twelve weeks. The group that had undergone LFA consistently showed significantly higher scores at that point in time in their rehab.

I showed these results to Brittany Dowling, a well-respected biomechanist currently working at Midwest Orthopaedics at Rush in Chicago, and she agreed that these early results showed good potential. "This is a great first step, but there are other tests I'd like to see—tuck jumps, drop jump, cutting using motion capture and force plates, even strength measures—but there's a lot of room for further research from here."

Another issue that is raised about the LFA is that while the procedure has shown good early results, there is very little published data. That kind of data takes years and while Lavender and others are starting to publish this, more research will be necessary.

Part of this is in the graft itself, where all the work on the tunnels and the protection by the InternalBrace doesn't make the transplanted tendon become a functional, living ligament any faster. Yes, the tendon actually changes at a cellular level, but those changes come in a four- to five-year period and nothing that is done in this or any surgery is known to accelerate that process.

Again, Dr. Lavender understands this line of thinking and agrees. "I would again say this is why we are studying this and in no way would we make a comment we certainly can bypass previous knowledge and return to play at three or four months at this point," he answered. "Our goal at this point is to study whether patients can return safely sooner than six months, but also understanding our technique only can add to the previous standard reconstructions because it is safe and doesn't add any complications."

While Dr. Lavender has focused on the knee and specifically the ACL with his procedure, I asked him if this could be used for other techniques. InternalBrace has been used extensively with ankles and elbows. Lavender wouldn't speculate on that possibility, given his focus both on knees as a specialty and on his practice in West Virginia. "We just see more knees," he explained.

Dr. Lavender used his technique on a local high school player named Devion Davis. Davis was a senior and highly recruited, eventually committing to West Virginia University. A scholarship is a big deal for anyone, but even more so for a young black man in West Virginia. In a game early in his senior season, Davis injured his knee, tearing his ACL and putting all of that in jeopardy.

He chose to have the fertilized ACL procedure done by Dr. Lavender and was ready for spring practice and for the start of his freshman year at WVU. The coaches at WVU saw early how well Davis was coming back and never wavered on his commitment, which often happens with injured players. This appeared to be a clear success for everyone.

Unfortunately, stories like this are anecdotal, but show both the potential and the risks of judging procedures like this. Davis made it back and started his football career at WVU, only to be felled by an autoimmune disease, causing him to get to dangerous blood counts. This obviously has nothing to do with his knee, but Davis's inability to continue with football could be considered a "failure" in some studies.

To be clear, this is very early days for LFA in terms of validation studies. Lavender acknowledges this and is excited that he's getting some of his first three-year studies done to go with some of the promising early results.

"A new procedure isn't going to have five- and ten-year studies," Lavender explained, "and people want that. I get it. The profession moves slowly for reasons, but what we've seen is promising. What really means the most to me is seeing these kids back on the field, doing what they love and getting a chance maybe they wouldn't have had."

Over and over, Dr. Lavender's procedure gets amazing reviews from the patients themselves, a fact that, while anecdotal in nature, cannot be ignored.

As more studies come out—and a major one for the LFA is the three-year study submitted in spring 2022—it will be interesting to see how quickly the surgery is integrated. There are other innovative techniques, from the InternalBrace ACL to the late Dr. Freddie Fu's "anatomic reconstruction" that he developed over years and has been widely adopted in European soccer.

Then again, who knows when something could go viral in the

modern world? "We had a patient who put out a video on TikTok," Lavender said with a laugh. "And we got a lot of calls. People quickly learned where Scott Depot, West Virginia was! We haven't marketed this. I've waited two, two and a half years to really get out and talk about this. I wanted the scientific process to take hold."

ILFA is a promising technique that bears further research. However, the real value of LFA or something like it that pushes the science of sports medicine forward isn't for someone like Jameson Williams, Odell Beckham, or any elite level player. They already get top-level care and while they lose a year of their career, it's seldom the career ender it was not so long ago.

It's in the possibility that a high school soccer player might not miss their senior season. It's in a college player not missing a year of their sports career, one they can never get back. Dr. Lavender and his procedure aren't just for pros. In fact, the strength of the procedure is in the very fact that it could work for anyone, anywhere.

If knees represent the weak point for any football player, the brain is what has come closest to ending football, not once, but twice. In the early days of football, the lack of any head protection led to a significant number of head injuries, including skull fractures and ultimately death. Almost a hundred years later, concussions and the long-term consequences of this misunderstood injury put the NFL and lower levels of football at a crossroads.

By 2022, concussions have ceased being an existential threat to the game, but remain a problem. The simple solution has always been to make a better helmet, but anyone that gives this answer is showing a basic misunderstanding about the problem. Simply put, the modern football helmet is not designed nor even capable of preventing concussion. It can reduce them, slightly, but the helmet is designed to prevent skull fracture and it's very good at that. Can you remember the last time a NFL or NCAA player had this injury? I looked through injury databases that cover the last decade and there was one. That injury happened when the player's helmet was knocked off and he continued in the play, being hit by another helmet when he had none.

(This is also a case where anyone that says rule changes can't happen quickly get pushed aside. After a single injury, the NCAA added a rule that a player that loses their helmet must disengage from the play or take a 15-yard penalty. That's right, they penalize the player that loses their helmet!)

The inherent tradeoff between preventing skull fractures and deaths, and reducing concussion is a tougher one. While there was never some sneaky, smoky-room meeting between the powers of football that said concussions were enough of a lesser evil, it's a delayed response. Concussions can be overcome and seldom create a real shock. Deaths on the field always do.

The NFL bought its way out of an existential crisis with concussions with a settlement in 2013 and finally approved by an appellate court in 2016. It was expensive, but now concussions are treated more like any other injury—mostly ignored, often treatable, but the player is replaceable. "Next man up" is more than a T-shirt slogan, but a reality for a game where very few players are truly irreplaceable.

Another innovation focused on the head was announced by the NFL's Medical Director, Dr. Allan Sills, in 2022 after a full year of testing its use. The NFL used machine learning to go through videos of every NFL play and came up with a "hit count," where every helmet contact was counted, whether that was to another helmet, a shoulder, or even a hit to the turf. Tests of the system show it is very accurate and reliable, which gives team medical staffs a new tool for managing workload during a season and perhaps suggesting technical changes to the coaching staff.

Scientists have attempted this kind of task previously, but it involves the drudgery of watching plays over and over again and subjectively counting impacts. Humans are bad at these tasks, but computer vision has progressed to a stage where it can do the job and never get tired or bored. Being able to get accurate information for every play in every game is a huge leap forward in data collection, but the question now is what the NFL will do with this data.

Their first step should be to share this technology, either by licensing it to NCAA and high school teams or better, creating a portal for teams to upload video and have it "head counted" for free. There's lots of questions about how the system actually works, so this may not be possible or may be much more complex than it would seem, but it's early days. If the NFL can get this system working for them, it's a big step forward. If it can get it working for the entire game, it's a huge leap forward.

We'll have to see if a hit count means anything more than a pitch count does in baseball. There's no clear way to tell if a hit is a hit, or if the force or direction of a hit is meaningful. Combining this kind of technology with baseline testing or some of the biomarker tests that are being developed is more likely to have a large impact, but there is hope that technology that's not that far down the road will lead to important changes and better data.

Spinal Injuries

While the head has gotten more attention in the last decade, the scariest injuries in football are spinal injuries. Neck and back injuries look brutal and cause delays on the field, leading many, especially the players, to have a moment of reflection that is problematic for the sport. While the NFL just simply runs commercials to cover, the sport at lower levels often doesn't have the medical coverage to minimize this.

There have been significant steps forward in the treatment of spinal injuries, but football's issue is preventing them. The problem since the beginning of the game is there's simply no good way to guard the neck or spine. There's no "spinal pad" and nothing short of an Iron Man suit is going to offer much in the way of real protection.

That means that instead of offering protection, the very type of activities that put the spine into risky situations have to be eliminated (see chapter on special teams).

The first note here is to recognize that not all situations that are treated as spinal issues are in fact spinal issues, or at least what we think of as the classic mechanisms and diagnoses. As it well should be, all issues that could be spinal issues are treated with the same level of care as if it were a significant spinal injury. So while it may look like a serious injury, it may also be something very transitory.

One of those transitory things is what's referred to as a spinal concussion. First diagnosed by Dr. Joseph Torg in 1986 as "cervical cord neurapraxia," this type of injury was a continuation of Torg's groundbreaking work on spinal injuries in the NFL. Torg had seen spinal injuries explode in the 1960s, largely, and perhaps ironically, due to the success of new football helmets.

The unintended consequence of better helmets (and the reduction in skull fractures and cerebral hemorrhages that went with it) were that players started doing things that were risky for the spinal cord. One of those was spearing—hitting directly with the helmet as the initial point of contact. The player would often throw himself and get arrow straight, hence the term "spear."

The NFL quickly dealt with spearing, making it illegal, up to the point of ejection, and continued to evolve its rules to try and cut down on these problems. Credit where credit is due, the NFL and football in general has been able to significantly reduce those spinal cord injuries. The problem is that any number means someone, usually a high school player, is left maimed and changed for life.

Over the last ten years, there has been a decrease in severe spinal injuries, but we have seen an increase in cervical cord neuropraxia, which is often called a "spinal concussion." With this, the spinal cord is shocked and for a moment, it shuts down, which can mimic para- or quadriplegia. The spinal cord rattle around in the space of the spinal column, much as the brain is thought to rattle around inside the skull. Luckily, the symptoms normally go away in a short period of time, though they can last for months or even linger to the point it appears permanent.

The best known case of this is Ryan Shazier. During a game in 2017, the Pittsburgh Steelers linebacker went headfirst into a low tackle and remained face-down after the play. It appeared that he could not move his legs and was pointing at his lower back. He was rushed to the hopsital quickly had what the team called "spinal stabilization surgery," which was later noted to be a fusion in his lower back, where a disc is removed and the vertebrae are fused together with a metal cage.

With Shazier, his initial issue was that the disc in his spine essentially exploded, causing a shock to the spinal column itself. It took months for Shazier to walk, which he did dramatically at the NFL draft about nine months after his injury. He was aided and halting, but walking nonetheless. A year later, he was jogging, but he never got back to a point where he could play again and retired from the NFL. Shazier is walking more normally now, but is not back to where he was prior to the injury and surgery.

Shazier's case is extreme. Most spinal concussions leave no lasting symptoms, but that makes them no less serious and certainly no less scary. That leaves us asking if, like skull fractures and concussions, we could create a reduction in them, and for what remains (or if reduction isn't possible), then how can we improve return to play?

Reduction should be possible. Changes to rules about hitting with the helmet have helped reduce neck injuries, which should trickle down. There's an effort, as detailed in the chapter on special teams, to remove many of the plays/chances for that injury to occur.

The bigger issue is that the treatment of this issue has learned over time that there's one significant detail that strongly factors into a return or whether a player should be playing at all. That is the width of the spinal canal itself. While the spinal column can be narrowed by many factors, a condition called spinal stenosis, many people simply do not have wide canals from birth.

In fact, this congenital condition is what ended the football career of Cooper Manning, the older brother of Peyton and Eli. Cooper was reportedly quite the quarterback himself, but elected not to play after he was diagnosed with the condition shortly after coming to Ole Miss. Peyton, who wore the #18 jersey in honor of his older brother, also had some severe neck issues later in his career, though he's never released if there were any congenital issues.

The spinal canal can easily be measured by MRI or even X-ray, but this is seldom done for youth or even college players due to the cost. Having this as a baseline could likely save many serious injuries or prevent the players at highest risk from even taking the field. While it seems harsh to deny someone with talent a chance, there are plenty of other sports to play, given that the cost might be the ability to walk or move any of his extremities.

One of the best known spinal injury cases was Chuckie Mullins, a player at Ole Miss who in 1989 went head-first into a tackle at Vanderbilt and fractured his spine. From that point on, he lost all feeling and control below the neck. He was airlifted out and was a quadriplegic, though his fight to come back to campus was noted nationally, including a visit from then sitting US President George Bush.

Mullins was able to return to campus, to go back into the locker room, and to see his Ole Miss teammates play. Unfortunately, Mullins suffered an embolism, a common issue in quadriplegics, and died less than two years after suffering his spinal injury. There is no question that it led to the death of a promising, charismatic young man.

Coliseum Drive on the Ole Miss campus was renamed Chuckie Mullins Drive shortly after his death and remains there as a tribute.

Luckily, Mullins's story is rare. The hope is that continued advances in both treatment and prevention will make sure that we don't have to change the names on any more campus streets again.

Heat Illness

Korey Stringer reported to the Minnesota Vikings training camp in August 2001 and hopes were high for him and the team. Stringer was entering his seventh season in the NFL and at age 27, he was likely at the peak of his career. He was 6'4, 350 pounds, a monster of a man and an intimidating blocker to face.

On the second day of camp, it was hot and sticky. Stringer, who had trouble making it through practices on the first day, made it all the way through the morning session, a hard two and a half hour practice led by offensive line coach Mike Tice. During that time, Stringer vomited at least three times. After practice, Stringer walked back to the air-conditioned locker room, but remained hot and dizzy, according to teammates' later reports.

Athletic trainers and teammates helped get Stringer to a car and he was taken to the local hospital. He lost consciousness somewhere between training camp and the emergency room. Less than twelve hours later, Stringer was dead, the victim of heat illness causing multiple organ failure.

Today, the Korey Stringer Institute at the University of Connecticut helps to study and educate people about the dangers of heat illness (which is the medically preferred term for what has often been called heat stroke, sun stroke, and other colloquial terms.) They've done amazing work, but each year we get more stories and more deaths. In 2019, Hezekiah Walters, a 14-year-old football player near Tampa, Florida, went to an optional football conditioning practice. Instead of getting in shape for the upcoming season, Walters died before he left the field, a body temperature of 104 ultimately recorded by the medical examiner. There was no medical staff on hand at the practice, only coaches.

Each of these deaths and hundreds more like them—according to the Korey Stringer Institute, since 1995, football has averaged three deaths and more than one hundred cases of severe heat illness a year—are absolutely and completely preventable.

Though neither author of this book is a doctor, we assert that there is a simple solution to all heat illness.

First, each and every athlete in football or any sport, especially those that function largely outside in the heat of the sun, should have trained medical personnel at practices and games. A majority of states have no law requiring this and even in states that do, an athletic trainer is often overworked, covering multiple teams at the same time. Even if football gets priority, they could be called away at precisely the time they are needed. Moreover, they can't take the time to monitor what can be as many as a hundred athletes just at football, as they should. In the case of Walters, the district had athletic trainers, but they were not in attendance at this "optional" practice.

Second, each of these athletes—again, in every sport—should have a thorough pre-participation physical, along with follow-up tests such as an EKG. While this is expensive, it's a lot cheaper than the million-dollar settlement that Hezekiah Walters's grieving parents were given.

Third, each athlete should be given proper time and guidance in how to acclimatize his or her self. Acclimatization is the process by which the human body becomes accustomed to physical activity in a new environment, normally one that is hotter and more humid. If the desired level of physical activity is intense, then the acclimatization process can take up to fourteen days.

The first stage of acclimatization (days one through five) involve improved control of cardiovascular function, including expanded plasma volume, reduced heart rate, and autonomic nervous system habituation, which serves to redirect cardiac output to skin capillary beds and active muscle. In the intermediate stage (days six through eight), the body begins to increase retention of salt—a factor in retention of electrolyte balance—and a fifteen to twenty percent reduction in exercising heart rate is accomplished.

During the final phase (days nine through fourteen), the plasma volume expansion begins to decay and is replaced by the longer-lasting reduction in skin blood flow that serves to increase central blood volume. Once this has been accomplished, the human body has made the adaptations necessary for healthy performance in the new environment. Acclimatization should be a scientific process, because we are dealing with the physiology of the human body. Larger athletes–especially those whose cardiovascular fitness level is questionable—and overweight athletes will not acclimatize as rapidly as smaller, more fit individuals.

Research has indicated that activity levels should be gradually increased during the acclimatization process, limiting strenuous activity to sixty to ninety minutes per day during the early stages, and that it is best to exercise during the morning or evening hours, when the temperature and humidity are lower than in the heat of midday.

Dehydration is another important aspect in heat illness, especially with larger athletes. The key factors are monitoring weight loss, hydration, and core body temperature. Weight loss is normally monitored by the use of weight charts. The athlete is weighed both prior to activity and after activity. The weights are recorded on a chart so that the medical staff can determine the athlete's exertion and hydration needs. Loss of as little as 2 percent of total body weight can lead to premature fatigue and impair mental status; losses greater than five percent can put the athlete at serious risk for heat illness.

Finally, and perhaps most simply, a person experiencing acute heat illness can often be saved by the rapid use of immersion in an ice bath. This is as simple as filling up a tub or an inflatable child pool with cold water and having ice available to put in. According to

Dr. Douglas Casa, the head of the Korey Stringer Institute and one of the world's leading experts on heat illness and its care, the proper treatment would be to cool an athlete "by any means necessary."

"Many teams have a simple Rubbermaid tub and ice near the field," said Dr. Casa. "At road races, we've had people literally walk away minutes after treatment." Many worry that an athlete being immersed in cold water would go into shock. Dr. Casa says this should not be a concern. "It's never happened. It's so much more important to cool the athlete as rapidly as possible, but we have no recorded instances of [shock] occurring in this manner."

This should also not be considered a medical treatment. It requires no training to fill a tub with ice and put someone in it. There's no need for anything more than a common sense assessment—"this man looks hot and doesn't seem healthy"—nor does it require a medical degree to monitor the person. In 2018, after the death of a football player at the University of Maryland, the athletic trainer said he did not put the player into an ice bath because he feared "he would drown." Man, hold his head and save a life. (The athletic trainer and several coaches were fired after an investigation.)

Dr. Casa detailed many factors that affect heat illness. These include overexertion, temperature, humidity, sun exposure, occlusive clothing (it is not unusual for individuals trying to lose weight to exercise while wearing a rubber or plastic jacket), dehydration, lack of acclimatization, concurrent illness such as an upper respiratory infection, and the use of any substance containing ephedrine.

The most important of these, he said, is humidity. "When you're looking at heat load, 70 percent of it is humidity. It's possible to have a relatively low temperature, but high humidity and be at a significant risk for heat illness." I asked if this put teams training in humid areas like the South at more of a risk than teams in more temperate climates, though even Minnesota and Wisconsin can get oppressively hot in the summer. "I've never seen any data on that, but it makes sense," he replied.

Heat illness has been recognized as a true medical emergency. It produces a marked hyperthermia that can cause widespread cellular damage. As stated earlier, the larger an individual is, the greater his exposure to heat illness will be. Unfortunately, it is not uncommon to hear of heatstroke fatalities at the start of preseason football, in hot, humid areas of the country.

Normally, an athlete is at risk for the exertional type of heat illness, where the exogenous heat load (determined by air temperature, humidity, and solar radiation) combines with the athlete's metabolism and muscle action to overwhelm the body's thermoregulatory system, creating an uncompensated heat stress. The evaluation at the practice site is usually based on changes in mental status (such as confusion or disorientation) and a core temperature greater than 105 degrees Fahrenheit. Of these risk factors, the ones that are within the athlete's control are the lack of acclimatization, physical fitness level, overzealous performance (competing above the individual's current level of fitness or ability), and dehydration.

Core temperature used to be best tested by rectal measurement, but this is uncomfortable for everyone, especially in younger age groups with untrained responders like a coach. Any measurement is better than none, but there's really no need. If someone reasonably suspects that a player is in distress, it's time to get the ice and dunk.

There have been new technologies that put a small pill-sized sensor into the body ahead of activities. They can be monitored wirelessly from a phone, allowing quick, accurate, and comfortable measurement, which can also give broad population ideas. Most heat illness is individualized and while most deal with the situation, sometimes one player doesn't, for whatever reason. The sensors are relatively cheap and pass through the system to be flushed away. (No, they're not reusable!)

Concurrent illness can play a factor in heat illness. Nobody wants to call in sick because they have a slight cold or minor influenza symptoms when they are trying to impress coaches and team personnel. However, symptoms such as fever and diarrhea can have serious effects on dehydration of the human body and put it at greater risk during physical activity in hot and humid conditions. This is obviously of even greater concern when there's been a pandemic of a respiratory virus, but this often happens with standard seasonal flu or common colds as well. There's also some question here in 2022 about whether "long COVID" will have an effect on any number of systems.

The use of occlusive clothing in the form of "sweat jackets" made of rubber or vinyl has been a mainstay around sports for years. The idea behind their use is that the athlete will sweat more during activity and therefore lose weight. That much is true. However, the weight being lost is the result of water loss, and that can lead to dehydration. Also, any weight lost in this manner will be regained as soon as the body is rehydrated.

Human body heat increases during exercise, but the body is normally able to dissipate heat and cool itself through the process of sweat evaporation. If this heat is trapped under an occlusive garment, then evaporation and normal heat dissipation cannot occur, therefore interfering with the body's thermoregulatory system and putting the athlete at risk for heat illnesses.

A final risk factor is the culture of football itself. Stories like the "Junction Boys," the early Texas A&M squad led by Bear Bryant that trained on a small farm in southern Texas in oppressive heat, all designed to toughen them up. Luckily for Bryant, he didn't kill any of the talent he had on that team or his legend might have been derailed. Too many coaches glorify "toughing it out," with many saying water breaks indicate weakness or using extra running as punishment rather than conditioning.

A player always wants to impress his coaches and teammates, but sometimes it goes too far. Players don't ask for help, pushing despite the fact that their bodies are screaming at them to stop.

Sometimes, it goes too far and the body betrays itself, unable to cool, and we're in a heat emergency.

All of these situations are avoidable, preventable, and even curable if the proper procedures are in place. If you're a coach, player, or parent, make sure you know what the plan is for your loved one's school or team, especially at lower levels where there is not a qualified medical staffer on hand at every practice. There never has to be another player felled like Korey Stringer, but there's more progress to be made.

Conclusion

The game of football has, since its inception, been a dangerous game. Injuries and even death were part and parcel of the sport back in the days of Teddy Roosevelt, Knute Rockne, and George Gipp. At the same time and often in parallel, sports science and sports medicine have made huge leaps forward, which have also helped society in general.

An ACL injury was once a career-ender. Now, it's a painful bump in the road, a lost year on the road to the Hall of Fame for Tom Brady, with advances that might make that lost time even shorter. Further advances across the sciences are helping with other injuries or even preventing them.

The game is never going to be perfectly safe, but it's clear that the sport can't go backwards either. Some trolls said that rules to prevent concussions would turn the NFL into a pale imitation of itself. The smart people inside the game are making sure that the best players are on the field more, using every tool they have and researching to make it even better. There will always be injuries in football, but the game should never be defined by it either.

EQUIPMENT

There's a trope in any football movie where the young player is handed his equipment. The helmet, the jersey, or the cleats often seem to be some symbol of "I made it!" and that now, they're part of something bigger. This scene in *Rudy*, the famous underdog story, is one of the centerpieces of the movie and yet, it seldom goes down this way.

From the start of American football, equipment has really been secondary. It's been the answer to an issue and a minimization rather than a leap forward in safety or function. While the modern football helmet is far safer than the old "leatherhead" helmets of yore, the function is largely the same. Everyone had something roughly similar and to change or to try and be more proactive is simply not in the game's DNA.

The basic premise of the helmet hasn't changed, even with major advances in material sciences, due to the success of the helmet at its intended purpose. Soft helmets would be better at padding the brain, but create more size and weight. Many teams use them in practice, often over a standard helmet, while 7-on-7 football has adopted a more advanced soft headgear that looks more like a boxing headgear than a football helmet.

There's been evolution, but into the early 2000s there wasn't much change. A bit of a shaping here and there, some new padding for comfort, but until the concussion crisis came for real in the mid-2000s, there wasn't much incentive and even then, several companies that made football helmets went bankrupt, in part to avoid the onslaught of lawsuits that came out at this point. That all led to the NFL's concussion settlement, which quieted things, but didn't really change much.

Helmets did evolve, largely due to some small changes and the threat of more lawsuits from lower levels. The NFL did put some money into research and frankly, it was a great investment to a point. Using third-party safety scores, usually from a Virginia Tech lab, helmets have gotten significantly safer over the last decade, in part due to grants and prizes awarded by the NFL. The league made investments in VICIS, a company with an innovative, high-scoring helmet. As a business, it needed a bankruptcy and a bailout, but the helmet itself was not only better, it led to innovation from entrenched companies like Riddell and Schutt, as well as innovation from outside.

Then there's the late Bill Simpson's Simpson-Ganassi football helmet, which unfortunately never caught on despite test results that showed it significantly better than existing helmets when introduced. Simpson, who passed away in 2019, will be best remembered for his work in auto racing, from helmets to fire suits, the latter of which he'd demonstrate by simply setting himself on fire. When he saw how big the problem was, he took his expertise to the back of his racing shop and built what he believed was a better helmet. Simpson's foam-based helmet interior not only protected the head more, it was significantly lighter. Go watch a Pop Warner game and the kids look like bobbleheads because the helmets they wear are made for far larger bodies. Their necks can't take the additional weight.

Both Simpson's and VICIS' helmets represented steps forward, but the nature of the game makes it only that concussions can be reduced by better accepting the forces of football, both the hits from other players and from the turf itself. Even teammates are a problem. In the 2022 AFC playoffs, star defensive back Tyrann "Honey Badger" Mathieu dove for a tackle and put his head in the way of a teammate's knee. Despite wearing a modern helmet, Mathieu was knocked unconscious and missed all but the first few plays of a very tight game. Mathieu's presence could have been a huge difference, given it went to overtime!

So, if better helmets can't help with concussions, can anything? The Food and Drug Administration approved the marketing of one device in 2021 called the Q-Collar. That approval stamped on the device hasn't slowed the controversy surrounding it, however. To be clear, the approval itself is controversial, only allowing the marketing of the device without endorsing it or even fully testing it.

The Q-Collar was developed by a company called Q30 Innovations and looks like a thick, C-shaped metal piece that goes around the neck with a small gap in front. The device applies noticeable pressure inward, essentially functioning as a choke collar that restricts blood flow to and from the brain. I've worn the device and the pressure is noticeable, but not uncomfortable.

The basic concept of the Q-Collar is that the brain has the ability to move around inside the skull and in a concussion, the brain is "sloshed" from side to side, causing trauma. That mechanism of injury help, called contrecoup, is controversial in and of itself, but what the Q-Collar does is try to hold more fluid in the brain, reducing that sloshing. Yes, that means pressure inside the head would be increased in theory, but not enough to cause any issues on its own.

Studies have shown that in football, there is some apparent effect, reducing concussions in one study with 284 13-year-old subjects. The control group, which did not wear the device, showed some changes in the brain apparent on MRI, while the group wearing it saw 77 percent of that group show no significant changes.

The Q-Collar costs $199 and is seeing some level of uptake in football, soccer, and a few other sports. More study is needed to see its effect, but there's been some early studies that do show positive results. The device is "FDA cleared," which is something short of approved, but something most products in this space never get.

David Myer, the Cincinnati-based inventor of the Q-Collar, thinks that the biggest effect will be on the military, where concussions from explosions were a major and ongoing issue in Iraq and Afghanistan, given the profusion of IEDs and other shock weapons. He told *Sports Illustrated* that "instead of adding external shells to the head, maybe we should be working at coming up with a better solution that protects it from the inside."

That's a pretty bold statement, but Myer has several studies that seem to side with him. In addition, several NFL players have worn the device in games, including Luke Kuechly, a linebacker who played several seasons with the Carolina Panthers. Kuechly, a Cincinnati native, had significant concussions throughout his career and wore the Q-Collar for the last few. While it's impossible to say whether or not the Q-Collar reduced the possibility of concussions, Kuechly did play 16 games in his next to last season after having the previous three ended by severe concussions.

While the Q-Collar has not seen significant uptake in the NFL, there is no restriction against its usage. We'll have to see if it becomes a part of more players' equipment in the future, but it's not the only collar out there purporting to help with head injuries.

Unlike the Q-Collar, the Kato Collar is a much bigger device which attaches to the shoulder pads. It's tough plastic with padding inside the collar that is designed to decelerate the head and helmet. Where its efficacy is most apparent is in slowing the head as it goes to ground, which can often be a whipping motion with a sudden stop as the helmet impacts the turf.

There have been previous collar add-ons in football, but those were designed to limit motion of the helmet and head to prevent neck injuries rather than purport to reduce concussion. At $250, the Kato Collar isn't cheap and doesn't have the kind of studies to back it that the Q-Collar does, but there is more adoption, with hundreds of teams using the device currently. We'll have to see if published studies are forthcoming, but as a pad adjunct rather than a de novo medical device, the Kato Collar doesn't need the same kind of approvals.

Another area where the on-field product is trailing the scientific progress is regarding rib issues. These are a common injury, especially to quarterbacks and wide receivers, though it can be seen at almost any position, especially at lower levels.

Unlike a lot of the other things in this book, we aren't looking to the future. While there's sure to be more improvements, football could do better in this case by adopting technology that's been around since the 2000s rather than the rough equivalent of the 1960s. That's right, rib protectors—often called flak jackets—haven't changed much in their most popular form since they were introduced.

Back in the 1960s, rib protectors were introduced, though it seems like several manufacturers brought them out at nearly the same time. In all the cases, they were extensions from the shoulder pads and were made of the same foam and plastic. That's essentially where we are in 2022 and there's simply no reason for it.

There are multiple brands of rib protectors on the market currently that use far more advanced materials, are lighter in weight and retain less heat, and offer significantly better protection. Two of the leading types are EvoShield and Unequal. The former used its form-fitted padding to produce what becomes essentially custom-fitted guards of all types including ribs.

The latter, Unequal from Philadelphia, uses kevlar and very thin foam to replace the standard plastic and foam. Their "Invincible" shirt features the materials in a comfortable compression shirt that can be worn under the shoulder pads and jersey. They've not only got lab tests, but are one of few products that has FDA clearance.

So why don't athletes use it? The usual discussion is about comfort and weight, but neither of those holds up given the product. Several quarterbacks have switched to Unequal after rib injuries, such as Tony Romo, and it is believed that Andrew Luck wore one after his kidney laceration, at least during practice.

For most padding and protection, the lack of change is simply a case of inertia. Most players won't switch from anything unless forced, even to the point of taking out pads. Watch any game and you'll see players that have removed the standard knee and thigh pads from their football pants. Others will use the smallest possible. This is often done by speed players, who would rather save a couple ounces than have protection.

There's simply no way to know if there's a higher rate of injury for players that have taken them out. There's no database that tracks what players remove those pads, or don't wear a rib protector, let alone a modern rib protector. Athletic trainers around the league probably have the data or at least an anecdotal sense, but these players are accepting a risk and are a role model for younger players.

The same was true with helmets, where players who had been wearing older helmets that did not meet standards fought to keep wearing them. Antonio Brown famously refused to practice in anything but his older helmet, though that was just one of many complaints Brown had in his short time with the then Oakland Raiders.

The removal of knee and thigh pads plus the inertia that players have with old, "comfortable," but outdated technologies are problematic, but in a league that is willing to fine players for sock height and untucked jerseys, they haven't taken a leadership position for safety. Even if only as a role model, there's a clear upside to this.

The same is even more true for the use of braces in the sport. The most visible are prophylactic knee braces. These are knee braces worn to prevent injury, rather than the more known brace designed to support an injured or rehabbing player with stability. In college football, several upper-level teams including Alabama, Texas A&M, Michigan, and Iowa require the use of prophylactic knee braces for every lineman.

However, we continually see players that just did a couple seasons in college with braces take them off when they get to the NFL. Even players that have suffered knee injuries take them off. Often players either question the effectiveness (despite extensive studies), question whether it slows them down (despite extensive studies), and just say they don't like wearing them. It's an accepted risk for adult, professional players to be sure, but again, there's little or no logic to be found here.

Braces have gotten lighter and stronger with materials like titanium and carbon fiber, but the uptake and use of prophylactic knee braces remains low in the NFL. There is hope that the continued development, including some using exciting nano-technology, will increase the use and reduce injury in the NFL.

At the same time, players have taken up other braces. The use of ankle braces isn't ubiquitous in the NFL or college football, but even at lower levels, the use of braces is more available than continued taping and re-taping. At the lower levels, the athletic trainer often isn't there for practice and more than half of high schools do not have a full-time athletic trainer for any sport, including football.

One interesting brace that has seen significant uptake is the elbow brace. In 2012, J.J. Watt dislocated his elbow on a play and had significant ligament damage as well. Since then, he's worn a custom version of a Donjoy Bionic II brace, which might surprise you costs less than $100 for the off-the-shelf version. Watt's isn't significantly different aside from the custom fitting for his XXL arms. There's also some pictures out there showing Watt with a Breg brace on, but this is basically a question of Coke vs Pepsi.

Watt was a superstar and Defensive Player of the Year at the time he started wearing the brace, but it quickly became acceptable for others to wear them. Some, like Richard Sherman, had injuries and have worn it since then to prevent further damage. Others seem to be wearing them prophylactically, hoping to borrow some cool or intimidation from being like Watt. Even at the pro level, wanting to look cool and following a role model is real.

Another intriguing area where the NFL and some major colleges have seen a way to reduce collisions is the use of robots. That's right, teams have robot tackling dummies that can move and dodge to replicate players. Some systems can actually run entire plays to simulate the opponent, which is often done with backups, the so-called "scout team."

Using the robots, which are basically really big Roombas with a foam-padded dummy on top, clearly reduces collisions. The scout team isn't getting hit and the player is hitting foam instead of a human. There are some issues. The dummies can't hand off or pass the ball, but some companies have come up with novel solutions. One variety uses lights on top to indicate the ball. The robot QB "hands it off" to the robot RB and the light goes red at the virtual transfer.

The major functional issue is speed. The robots aren't up to simulating a Kyler Murray or Tyreek Hill at this stage and one coach I spoke with that used them says they're great for "walkthroughs, basically. You're jogging, not running." That's sure to change as technologies develop.

The other is cost. These are not cheap, and they require maintenance and someone to run and set up the system. That's easy for NFL teams or major colleges, but well beyond the means of most lower levels. Even at the NFL level, the newness and strangeness of using robots has held back the adoption.

One of the leading manufacturers of this kind of robot is Mobile Virtual Players, referred to as MVP. Their version of a football robot runs about $1,000, but it's six feet tall and weighs about 185 pounds, which is a reasonable replication of size. It runs about a five-flat 40-yard dash and can top out at twenty mph. Maybe MVP isn't a first-round pick, but again, it's a reasonable simulation.

The MVP was developed at Dartmouth, in anticipation of the Ivy League's rule change that eliminated contact in practice, starting in 2016. Some students noticed that the rule prohibited contact between players, but not on a robot, and the process started.

In 2017, the Pittsburgh Steelers became the first NFL team to try out a full MVP setup, which cost about $8,000 at the time. Head coach Mike Tomlin told the media that he loved the robots. "They don't get tired and they're always ready," he said.

Several other teams have tried them, but as yet, there's not a wide adoption at any level. There's no clear answer as to why—they work, they're not out of the cost realm for any upper-level team, and they're getting better at replicating a player. This might end up being one of those products that will take generational change, that an old-school coach might never accept. It's also true that teams don't value their lower-level players, seeing them as easily replaceable, so why spend money on a robot when the practice squad player is right there?

MVP as a company has branched out, using the same technology for the training of military and police. Their MVP robot can be outfitted to move and dodge like a suspect or opponent would, or to charge someone aggressively, something a simple range target can't do.

There's a ton of promise with robots, but there's a couple problems. The first is the simple cost. There's a lot of money in football, but it's at the upper levels—the NFL and major colleges—where it can actually do the least good. Add in that these upper levels tend to be very conservative and not want to spend money or integrate technology and a small market becomes even smaller. Getting the cost down is difficult if the top level isn't funding growth and scale.

Hope for technologies like this are going to come from lateral connection. Robot manufacturers could use a small, unprofitable, but very noticeable market in the NFL to show and test their technology, then use the marketing to launch into other markets. There's also likely to be some trickle-over, as a robot built for a warehouse loading and unloading operation could be changed to create a tackling robot as it nears the end of its usable life and gets donated to a local college or high school.

Checking the Turf

Back in 2015, Tim Newcomb of *Sports Illustrated* created a ranking of NFL stadiums. He rated Indianapolis' Lucas Oil Stadium as number 13 (of 32) and paid special attention to the FieldTurf Classic HD artificial surface at the stadium.

In 2016, Zach Binney, an epidemiologist, published the results of his study of injuries in stadiums and Lucas was at the tail end of the rankings, showing far more foot, ankle, and knee injuries than other stadiums. Binney's groundbreaking study was widely cited and noticed, including in Indianapolis, where the turf was switched to Shaw Sports Turf's Momentum Pro in 2018.

Part of this is how the turf is maintained, especially in a multi-use stadium like Lucas Oil, which is connected to the Indianapolis Convention Center and regularly used for conventions, events, and concerts, as well as other sporting events like soccer and motocross.

Binney's study hasn't been replicated since his initial collection and publication, and injury data is hard to come by in the NFL. Overall, injuries on turf have continued to be higher, but this is more a census than a study of why this is occurring or any specific mechanisms.

Lucas Oil Stadium is far from alone, but many players have taken note of it. Santonio Holmes said that turf ended his career and that Jameson Williams, who sprained his knee on the Lucas Oil turf early in the 2022 College Football Playoff National Championship Game, was a victim of it. Ahmad Bradshaw told this author in 2014 that he felt the turf was inconsistent. Bradshaw was coming back from a Jones fracture in his foot and he felt that it would go from "too bouncy one day, too hard the next." While he didn't blame the turf alone for problems with his foot, he made it very clear that it didn't help.

The Colts' medical staff has made progress with injuries, improving over the last several years, which makes it a bit tougher to isolate for the turf. Anecdotally, it is still not well liked, with players like Derrick Henry (fractured foot) and the Colts themselves having several unusual foot and ankle injuries. Some of these came at the Colts training facility, which uses an identical turf.

Other studies, such as one done by the Hospital for Special Surgery, show the increased risk of certain injuries on turf is offset by the decreased risk of others. As well, grass isn't an instant fix. In most cases, it comes down to maintenance. This is another area where at the NFL and college levels things are fine, but we see more problems with poor and poorly maintained surfaces as we go down the line. Our youngest, most vulnerable players are often playing on the worst surfaces.

Surprisingly, it's tough to get good results because turf is very different from stadium to stadium, even before accounting for age and maintenance. In the 2021 season, there were six different manufacturers of turf and most of those had multiple types of turf. FieldTurf had four different kinds on the four fields it covered with none the same!

One theory that I have had since the mid-2010s and that players, coaches, and medical staff have agreed with to some point is that while this is likely some fault of the turf, it's quite possible that it's because the turf is too good. It's too "sticky" and doesn't give in the same way as grass/dirt does.

The injury called "turf toe" is a sprain of the big toe that first was noticed on early turf. Because that was essentially carpet over concrete, there was little or no give and players would not dig into the dirt with their cleats as normal, causing a hyperextension and injury to the ligaments.

This type of issue has been known since a 1992 study at the University of Iowa, after a rash of injuries on the school's new turf fields in several sports. The combination of turf, maintenance, and shoes was found to be the issue and finding that balance was supposed to be the next step. However, that's difficult since most athletes have very strong opinions about shoes and both shoes and turf have seen huge performance gains from that point to now.

In effect, turf that has too high a coefficient of friction ("too sticky") is combined with shoes that also have a high coefficient of friction, as well as other performance features including reduced weight and additional support. A 2019 study done in part by Dr. Robert Anderson, one of Green Bay's team doctors and a regularly consulted surgeon for lower leg injuries, concurs, calling it a "bio-mechanical hypothesis" that the fact that the turf doesn't release the shoe quickly changes the biomechanics of movement, resulting in the increased injuries. While this study wasn't definitive and couldn't prove out the hypothesis, the 16 percent increase in lower extremity injuries was seen as causal. (That's bad.)

One of the issues that led to turf fields is that domes, even retractable domes, don't make great places to grow the kind of high-quality grass necessary for a field. Several stadiums, starting with State Farm Stadium in Phoenix, began putting in "trays"—large, movable systems that could bring grass inside for game days, then back out to the sun for the other times. For systems in Phoenix and Las Vegas, this is difficult due to heat and lack of rain, but again, resources aren't a problem for teams. It's amazing that they'll spend millions on keeping grass green in the desert, but not on figuring out why there's so many lower leg injuries putting their athletes on the sidelines.

All that and in the Super Bowl in 2022, the Rams nearly lost the game when Odell Beckham Jr, one of their star wide receivers, sprained his ACL for the second time in his career. He was running a simple crossing route, caught his foot, and collapsed to the very turf that potentially caused the injury. We've seen this again and again, not just in big games, but in far too many games at every level.

Conclusion

The basic equipment for football has evolved, albeit slowly. The game now is safe, but could be safer with the mere use of the best possible equipment, especially at lower levels, where cost is the major concern. Youth pads and helmets are often hand-me-downs or generations behind, besides being engineered for larger players.

There's progress to be made at both ends. Football as a sport could do more simply by accepting and using existing technologies, but those technologies often have high hurdles in order to gain even a toehold at the upper end of the market. On the other side, American sports puts very little value in getting better technologies to lower levels, often leaving many younger and less economically advantaged youth exposed.

Consider the simple helmet. Not even the worst program can play without them, but most will play with older helmets that have been "reconditioned" several times. That phrase can mean a full manufacturer rebuild and replacement of worn padding, but in others, it can simply mean it's cleaned. Liability on school districts and youth programs hasn't been decided as it has at upper levels, so this is an area where doing even a little more could help grow the game at the same time it is made safer.

There is much more to be done. Low-hanging fruit like simply wearing it is available, while investment in the future has been shown to clearly get big results with even relatively small investments. While it is not a simple solution, it's not so hard to see where this could get better. The game deserves it.

TRAINING/DEVELOPMENT

There is something of a nature versus nurture argument in football. On the one hand, a look around any high level football team, even down to the high school level, shows that there's an amount of self-selection. Whether it's regarding speed, aggression, or sheer size, football players are not normal. Spend a week at the NFL Combine and you'll see the extremes of the physical form and physical talents.

Those same athletes are training at the extremes, pushing their bodies to the limits. Some will break down under this load and others will excel. The NFL, and even lower levels, showcases the purest survival of the fittest. It's not just the playoffs where it's win or go home.

In east Texas, the home of Hall of Famer Earl Campbell, it looks like two men are playing a kid's game. There are two circles of small cones in a figure eight. They start at opposite ends, one trying to catch the other. They run, stop, and burst. They switch from one side to the other, from slide steps to sprinting, and make it look effortless. After a few seconds of this high-intensity tag, the chaser finally tags the chasee—Chiefs quarterback Patrick Mahomes. The former MVP and Super Bowl winner smiles, but also looks down. He's not happy with losing.

After a few rounds of others playing, Mahomes is back up. This time he's smoother, faster, and the chaser gasses out before getting him. Mahomes is a top-level NFL player, one of the most evasive quarterbacks in history, so this shouldn't be surprising. However, Mahomes is just a few months out from ankle surgery, the injury that made him so much less mobile on their run to the Super Bowl and contributed to their loss to Tom Brady's Buccaneers.

It's hard to imagine Brady, the last of the pocket passers, doing

Mahomes and Ehlinger training with Bobby Stroupe at APEC in Texas.
Photo courtesy Stroupe/APEC.

this drill. Mahomes darts, drifts, and spins, leaving his drill partner gasping for air, flailing as a desperation dive comes up short. Mahomes is laughing and I can only imagine that he's visualizing running this against defenses that will think they have him, only to be left with air, watching Mahomes spin away and launching another touchdown pass.

I first went to Bobby's facility, known as APEC, back in 2016 and the training I saw there was astounding. That facility, just outside Fort Worth, was attached to a sports facility, which had a Texas-sized number of basketball and volleyball courts, as well as a medical office for Ben Hogan Sports Medicine, one of the top orthopedic practices in the area.

The beautiful facility has a huge turf field, marked for sprinting, drills, and distances for throwing sports. There's all sorts of equipment, weights, and technology, but the thing that stood out for me, watching the instructors take a group of pro athletes through a hard workout, is that they all seemed to be having fun. On any given day, there could be a handful of NFL quarterbacks, like Mahomes, Jalen Hurts, or Sam Ehlinger, plus a group of MLB pitchers, like Michael Kopech, who's been clocked at 105 mph with his fastball.

Even more unusually, these pro athletes don't get more attention than anyone else in the facility, down to a group of elementary school kids. APEC trains kids down to kindergarten, but don't get the idea that Stroupe has a factory churning out pro athletes. As important to him is training everyone equally, down to his "APEC Adaptive" program, which has this mission statement on the website:

The APEC Adaptive Foundation provides training systems, experiences, and overall support for kids, athletes, adults and veterans affected by, but not limited to: spina bifida, amputation, brain injury, military injury and poverty. Our purpose is to provide adaptive services free of charge to all participants.

It's a long way from where Stroupe started out, opening his own facility after having managed a large fitness club and realizing he didn't want to sell gym memberships. Even that was a bit of a Plan B, after Stroupe spent a year playing for the Wichita Falls Thunder, an Arena Football League team, which only won one game before folding shy of the end of the season.

Stroupe ended up setting up his first practice with a sports medicine group in Tyler, Texas, about an hour and a half east of Dallas. It's not a small town, but aside from the aforementioned Earl Campbell, who graduated from John Tyler High School in 1973, this wasn't where you'd expect one of the top performance training centers to exist.

However, flowers grow where they grow, and APEC popped up in the Rose City. Stroupe explained that the sports medicine group had heard about his work with some local athletes. "The athlete that had spoken highly [of me] was Matt Flynn, who ended up going to LSU and doing some things, but he was a high school kid when I worked with him." Some things, indeed. Flynn won a national championship as LSU's starting quarterback in 2007 and went on to an NFL career that lasted eight years.

Stroupe expanded on what he'd been hired for quickly. "They [the clinic] just wanted someone to work with people that needed a bridge between what their insurance would cover for physical therapy and when they were able to return to play. We were just gonna run what we called 'speed camps' in the summers. I didn't even have a name for the place, and we call it 'Accelerate.' Then Accelerate turned into "performance enhancement center" after we got a little garage building behind the PT clinic. That got shortened to APEC, just so people didn't have to say the whole darn thing!"

Grow it did. Stroupe sounded humble as he detailed that growth. "It's been a real blessing. I have a great team and I've had a lot of great clients. We went from training in public parks and having thirteen people in my first program to now, we probably service about six thousand people a year and we have over 250 pro athletes across six different sports. It's been a lot of fun. It's been really something, man. I never wanted to be in business. I didn't have ambitions for that. I just wanted to help kids that were like me—the small kids that got picked on and that was kind of my mission, and it just kind of grew organically."

One of the things that helped this growth was a philosophy, one that's painted on the wall and printed on T-shirts today. "Our mantra is 'Be the Best You.' I think the first thing we have to do is find out who our athletes are. Most of these sayings can come off pretty hollow, but for us it's a defining statement. We have to investigate who our athletes are. You're not going to get that from just doing some assessment on a singular day or even across a week. It requires a lot of focus and vision to learn your athletes. You can't define every weakness and every strength. and you got to be able to visually see it sometimes and act on it and coach it.

Coaching is such an art. I don't like to try to get everybody to be certain standards. I just think even in a team setting, even in a group setting, individualization of how things are actually done is incredibly important."

While Stroupe's programs are very individualized, he is still best known today for his work with one individual, Patrick Mahomes, the Super Bowl-winning QB of the Kansas City Chiefs. Stroupe and Mahomes have been working together for a long time. "I've worked with him since he was a fourth grader," Stroupe told me. "You know, we didn't do personal training stuff. He was just in my groups. When he got into high school, we started doing some things a little more closely, but he's still in the groups 80 percent of the time. You know, I'll be honest, I had forgotten about that until he referenced it at the Pro Bowl one year. I didn't remember."

Mahomes grew up in the area, the son of Pat Mahomes, a longtime reliever in Major League Baseball. Tyler, Texas was a bit off the beaten path, but things certainly went well for Patrick. He was a star athlete and found a coach that he's worked with going on two decades. Just because Stroupe doesn't remember some of those group classes with the youths doesn't mean Mahomes didn't eventually stand out. It's just not likely in ways that you'd imagine.

"As far as what makes him special, there's too many things. Patrick truly enjoys the challenge of getting better," Stroupe said thoughtfully. "He's been really good to himself from a standpoint of . . . you know, some people can never be happy with what they have. Patrick's always been really good about being confident in the gifts that he has, instead of wishing he had different gifts. Patrick wasn't the fastest kid, he didn't jump high. He didn't do the things that flash or pop in the weight room. Patrick Mahomes would be in the bottom third of almost everything you test for, but things like agility came when he was in high school."

That isn't to say Mahomes wasn't athletic, but that he went about it in an unorthodox fashion. "When you look at him, he's just a very unique athlete. I think the the only athlete that is comparable to him, athletically, in another sport right now is Luka Doncic, because Luka to me is the Patrick Mahomes of basketball. The reason I say that is because he's just unorthodox from the standpoint of how we define what an athlete is or what a good athlete can be good at. Patrick's spatial awareness, his visual perceptual abilities, his ability to display speed and power in a multitude of different vectors is just incredibly unique. It makes him an incredible challenge to work with, but also a lot of fun to work with."

That lack of orthodoxy also comes to the religion of Texas, football. It's not surprising that Mahomes excelled at baseball, as did his father, since both were blessed with excellent arms. More surprising is that it may have been his best sport for a while. One could imagine a coach taking the easy road and directing Mahomes to the sport his father played.

Stroupe can explain why that didn't happen. "Genetically, he's more gifted for baseball, I think, Well, I think football today, Patrick's changed the game a lot. I think he's changed a position. It's unique and different. The opportunities and the situations he's had allowed him to express himself in, in through this position in a way that he couldn't have done in baseball. In baseball, you can only be so creative on the mound.

There was another issue as well. "You know, I love Patrick, but he was having a hard time throwing strikes," Stroupe said with a laugh. "If you throw 93 miles an hour and top at 95, but you can't throw strikes, you're not a high draft pick. I think for Patrick, he realized that he's a creative person, he realized that he has incredible vision. He had good balance and he can throw from different places in high school. It didn't take long to realize that his future in football may have a higher ceiling than baseball. I mean, that was very apparent."

I asked Stroupe about that stunning figure eight drill. Was

it something he did with all his athletes and was Mahomes just singularly good at it? Stroupe thinks it's the way Mahomes moves and thinks. "If you look at his his capability and the way Patrick prefers to solve problems, he likes to loop because he's faster in a loop than he is straight, especially when he has any momentum. It's kind of like if you're on a motorcycle, you don't box a turn. He understands the momentum very well as a mover and he utilizes momentum. So the drill you saw with him, in that we do curvilinear work with him twice a week, because that's a big part of his game."

Stroupe may come off as *aw-shucks* at times, but his use of "curvilinear" in this context caught me off guard. This wasn't some variation on Rocky chasing a chicken while Mick yelled. This was science, a designed drill to create chaos and force a specific motion.

Stroupe continued. "We do curvilinear and semi-circle patterns at least twice a week with him, because that's how he plays. That's his best movement strategy. That's what he likes. He's really good at changing direction and agility as well, but that's a really good one for him, because it helps him utilize his momentum. He throws really good on those curves."

Stroupe used this drill, one he'd done a hundred times with Mahomes and with his other athletes. It's not an uncommon drill at APEC, though I've never seen it anywhere else in exactly this form, this uberathletic duck-duck-goose. "What I wanted to prove to him was that he's ready to play the game and play it the way he likes to play it. What I needed to do was more of a proving ground thing. When I saw him use a movement strategy that I know was familiar to him and that he likes to do, I knew that we were in a good place. The kid that was working with him was a defensive back that started games at TCU. So it wasn't like a defensive lineman that's usually chasing him. I mean, he made the kid look silly, but he's Patrick Mahomes! He does that. People don't realize he's out there beating three and four guys, and no team puts a slow player on him when they spy him."

That's a long way from a kid that didn't stand out in group classes.

For a coach, having a single athlete with success, let alone a Super Bowl ring and an MVP trophy, can be the basis of more success or at the very least, more volume of people willing to come and pay to train with that coach. That can be a double-edged sword. One can quickly see which coaches were lucky to have a great athlete magically appear, and which really helped. Think how few players stay with a coach for that long, in any sport, especially when they have the choice of anyone in the world, or even not paying for it at all.

With Stroupe and his team at APEC, they not only have created other quarterbacks that play at high levels, they've done it with very different kind of athletes. Jalen Hurts isn't Patrick Mahomes, nor is Sam Ehlinger or Mac Jones. If you're not reading this in 2022 or can't call it up in your VR viewer, Hurts is bigger and slower, while Ehlinger is a bit of a in-betweener that was questioned whether he could play in college and again in the pros. Mac Jones is a first-round pick, a national champion at Alabama, one of a tradition of quarterbacks that includes Joe Namath, Ken Stabler, and Tua Tagovailoa, whom he replaced after injury. Jones is a pocket passer more along the lines of Tom Brady, which is why the Patriots used a first-round pick to get Jones in.

With all those different quarterbacks—and again, these are just the ones at the pro level—I asked Stroupe how he deals with the differing styles. "We have our core tenets and our principles, our things that are non-negotiable. There's certain boxes you have to check. What sport? What position? What are their physical attributes? How do they like to play the game?" Stroupe says, ticking off those boxes with his fingers as he speaks. "Then you develop plans for them and you devote a percentage of your time to those things."

Stroupe continues, his hands and eyes darting as he grows more excited talking about the things he loves. "I think with quarterbacks, it's a lot of fun because they get to interpret that position in the way that they want to play it. There's probably no other sport besides basketball, with a point guard, that has the opportunity to create a persona and the way that you want to play it yet still be successful within the confines of this system. If you look at Patrick, look at Hurts and Jones and Sam, they're vastly different. But there's also a lot of things that are the same. It's kind of like flavors of ice cream. I like strawberry ice cream, but some people think it sucks. That doesn't mean it's the truth, but that's how I look at quarterbacks—there's a lot of good ways to do it. That's why who's coaching you and what your personnel is, and what your system is, is so important for a quarterback."

While Stroupe is at the top of his profession, one of the things that stands out is his commitment to all his athletes, and he uses a very broad definition that takes in his adaptive athletes and children all the way down to kindergarten. There may not be another Patrick Mahomes in one of the groups, but they all get the same level of coaching. It's almost like if Andy Reid, the head coach of the Kansas City Chiefs, went out on his free time and coached a junior high team.

I asked Stroupe why he thought that was important, and if he thought that kids in places that aren't Tyler, Texas, might not be so lucky to have someone there. Especially with economically disadvantaged or even rural youth, the opportunity isn't there without dollar and time commitments that many parents simply can't make.

He agreed. "That's true. I think that we need to rethink and reevaluate what youth football is. What are we doing? What is the goal mentally and physically? From an experience standpoint and coaching standpoint, I think there's a lot of things we can do at the lower levels and at the middle school levels to make football better. I've had ideas, but people want to win, and I think winning is just not that important until you're a varsity athlete." Parents around the state of Texas, try to contain your shock.

"If I had it my way, no one would have a set position until they're in high school. There'd be mandatory rules on having to play different positions and different sides of the ball, virtually every quarter until they were a high school athlete," Stroupe continued. "I think that if you truly want to love and know the game of football, you need to learn different positions. This has been proven in coaching—you want a head coach that's coached almost every position. But only the Patriots and a few other teams seem to value that."

Stroupe thinks this kind of approach could help football in more than just developing players, but solving another crisis. "I just think that that would be a really, really good way to develop better football players, that it would be better for the game, and create better coaches. There's so many people up in arms about diversity in coaching and things like that. Well, I think one of the biggest problems with diversity and coaching is some of these kids have only played one position their whole life, and then they want to be head coaches. That's an incredible disadvantage."

Watching Stroupe and his team coach, there's certainly a value on measurement and data, even without it being obtrusive. Stroupe can seem a bit old school in ways, but there's a lot of hidden ways that Stroupe is evaluating and he doesn't shy away from technology when he feels it adds something valuable. It's getting to that value that he feels is difficult.

"Data is starting to make its way into football, but it hasn't became useful yet. I think it will. Some teams are doing a great job with it. With some teams, it's just so much noise. Worse, it's just another box to check that it's there. It's getting in the way," Stroupe explained, but it's clear he's not against it. "I think there's a lot of value there in the right situation. Look, if you have a head coach that doesn't want to hear it and doesn't want help making decisions, I don't think it's going to be helpful. On the flip side of that, if you're letting technology people and analytics people take the place of the human element in the art of coaching, you're messing that up too, because it's not meant to take the place of the skill and talents of coaches. It's meant to be an asset to them."

"I think one of the easier things to look at is GPS numbers and all these different things. The problem is when people are using these as green light, yellow light, and red light. That's the wrong way to interpret this data. I think it's more of a way for you to decide how you want to coach these athletes and how to get the most out of their abilities. I think that until you get the position coaches, strength coaches, medical staff, the GM, and the owner on the same page with technology, it's not going to be of any value. If only one group is looking at it and having discussions over it, it's not going to do much for the organization," Stroupe says emphatically, slamming his hand down on his desk.

It's up for science and technology to prove itself to successful coaches and organizations, not vice versa. However, if you read into what Stroupe says and how he says it, he's hungry for information that will help him take his athletes even further, and that could be coming soon, even from a technology he says hasn't shown its value yet.

The Metabolic Cost of a Yard

In the metaphoric land war that is the game of football, every yard means something. At least, every yard forward means something, while every yard backward means the opposite. However, imagine one of those plays like Patrick Mahomes makes. He drops back, he scrambles out of the pocket, he cuts away from another defender, cuts upfield, and slides for a gain of a couple yards. He ran 40 or 50, but the marker only moves five yards up the field, halfway to a first down.

Plays like this happen all the time, often by design. Every end around or toss sweep is designed to use lateral motion to eventually find a vertical opening. You've probably seen players after a play calling for water or even finding the oxygen tank by the bench. There's a clear cost to each and every yard, but it's a metabolic cost. How much does a yard literally take from a player?

This is actually calculable and is a very important figure. In recent years, the NFL has begun giving us some information. Mahomes actually wore a heart rate monitor in games during the 2021–22 playoffs, allowing his heart rate to be shown after the fact. We've seen similar technology used in other sports, most notably auto racing. With just a bit more data, this is easily calculable. The NFL doesn't use either of the top location-based monitors during games, instead using a different technology called Zebra. However, both StatSports and Catapult are used during practices and in other ways by teams in the NFL, college, and many other sports.

Gary McCoy was the senior applied sports scientist for Catapult after spending years in professional sports. (*Full disclosure: Will Carroll works with McCoy at Northstarr at the time of writing.*) Gary offered some advice regarding how these technologies work.

"First, you deal with load—how much an athlete is doing. That's the easy part, tracking them and getting the raw data," McCoy explained. "Then you have to get into the calculated areas, like metabolic response, which is really looking at how an athlete is doing gas exchange and caloric utilization without actually measuring that specific athlete. That functional economy can be calculated from a number of studies and models, but remember that it's responsive to the musculoskeletal load, which is tactically decided within the environment by the demands of the sport."

Without getting too far into a very complex calculation, the basics of it have been widely tested in soccer, rugby, and other European sports, as well as track and field. The calculation involves components like the number and intensity of sprints, decelerations, and the time when metabolic load is high, as defined by a power to weight ratio. It is largely based on the work of Cristian Osgnach, an Italian sports scientist specializing in high-level soccer, who conducted a 2010 study showing that metabolic power correlated to VO2 Max, a common way of studying metabolic efficiency in the lab. (Ever seen a guy running on a treadmill and breathing into a tube? That's likely what's being tested.)

One of the things that's most difficult to understand at first glance is how decelerations are as key as accelerations. For this, you have to go back to how the game of football is actually played. It comes in starts and stops, cuts, and change of directions. All of those avoidance techniques are largely forms of decelerations and if a player can't change direction quickly, he's going to get hit, a lot.

Jo Clubb, a sports scientist that previously worked with the Buffalo Bills, wrote an article for *Sportsmith* in early 2022 that detailed how these decelerations could be measured and how undervaluing them in workload management has left many athletes overloaded and exposed to hundreds of motions that often cause injury. Think again of the 2022 Super Bowl injury to Odell Beckham Jr. He stopped and twisted, with his foot catching just a bit too much on the turf. His tibia shifted forward with the stop, overloading the ACL, and now he's got a new ligament and an off-season of rehab.

McCoy explained this in detail, but summed up well how it becomes functional to a football player, coach, and team. "We have known for years that deceleration rates and events are keys to overall load costs and need to be weighted as such. It's the breaking strain per yard—especially on pivots, cuts, turns, change of direction, and especially asymmetrical change of direction. Ironically, trunk stiffness is the gating factor to ensure repeatable deceleration management." There's an interesting action point, especially for lower levels.

Combining the workload with the known factors of metabolic necessity—oxygen and food—we're faced with the two ways that teams have to try and re-load players during a game. Supplemental oxygen would seem the easiest vector to improve this, but there's also an oxidative stress that occurs with this. Not only is oxygen necessary for life and for functioning on a football field, it can also do some things that aren't as helpful, much in the way that exposure to oxygen can cause certain metals to rust.

The better way is to get the body to process oxygen more efficiently, which is what most of us just call "getting in shape." It's tougher to create gains in elite football players, who are in great shape, but are not often elite oxygen processors. Football is a game of bursts; there's about seven minutes of action in a game, with most athletes moving less than ten yards on any given play. Long runs are highlights, rare things even for receivers and defensive backs. According to NextGenStats, the longest play in the NFL in 2021 was a 137-yard effort by Jakeem Grant, who was returning a punt. He went 40 yards longer than the 97 he's credited with on the scoresheet!

Once a team knows the output, then everything must turn to the input. In an anaerobic sport, with only occasional longer sprints, there shouldn't be a "gassed." You'll often hear announcers saying that "the defense has been on the field too long, they're tired now" or that a big running back "wears down a defense and gets better in the fourth quarter." These are demonstrably false.

A better analogy than sprints is an Olympic lift. For ease, let's call it a squat, since much of the line play is essentially this (with hand fighting and leverage) and it's not the worst proxy for runners sprinting for a few seconds on each play. That means a football game is a series of squats with random weights, ranging from near zero (players do take plays off) to a one-rep max (1RM).

In this proxy, a player would have to do one of these squats for every play. Using Super Bowl LVI, played in 2022, Aaron Donald played an extraordinary number of snaps, being in the game for 58 of 61 defensive plays. How was his energy? I'm sure he was tired, but his pressure of Joe Burrow at the end of the game—as near a sack as can be—showed he still had the ability to overcome double-teams and run down a mobile quarterback.

Remember as well, the game came after a two-week break and had an extended halftime that would allow rest and re-fuel. However, there's often more than even just the in-game load. McCoy told me a story about an elite athlete who was hurting himself with his routine, almost literally. While McCoy used the names, I've removed them to protect the innocent.

"Cost per yard was a feature of a discussion I had with an NFL team in 2015. Their star wide receiver was coming off a career year and had a hamstring injury when I got to their camp. He reported to camp late because he had just signed a big contract and he was doing everything he could to catch up. He was clearly overloaded and then the hamstring strain hit. But how? The easy answer is to nurse him back gradually, but during this time, I was working with the team's director of football research. We were able to see game day data from Catapult and it was surprising," McCoy told me.

"The head coach confirmed with me his belief that when the game counted the most, in the fourth quarter after 12 to 17 plays on offense, the wide receiver's speed and effectiveness were way down. He could see that he was gassed and the data showed the coach was right. When we unpacked the player load data from the 100 percent he had available in load on game day, a whopping 40 percent was coming from his pregame warm up!" said McCoy with a laugh.

"You can't go in and take that away from the athlete," McCoy continued, explaining the challenge of making the data meaningful in a game where this player had just received a $20 million signing bonus and more in guaranteed money on a five-year deal. "Warmup is ritual. It's superstition. We had to break down for him all the things he was doing that were just eyewash. He had twenty-four elements to the routine and we showed him the load cost of each. We could show him what each element was taking out of his personal gas tank, fuel that could be used later."

The player returned to play, but was felled by a fracture,

something that all the monitoring couldn't help. (For more on turf injuries like this, see the chapter on equipment.) However, being able to change the player's routine was a huge win for McCoy and the system. In most situations, that wouldn't be possible, and it's some credit to the player that he was willing to listen.

McCoy thinks the implications from this kind of analysis are huge for the game. "Armed with that kind of data, any coach and his performance staff could ideate a 'full gas tank movement blitz' late in the game. This could functionally alter the play calls and even the personnel package designs with one goal: 100 percent availability at those key moments at the end of the game. Real time cost mapping or fatigue monitoring could factor into every single decision made. It could be the 'Carfax' for teams and coaches, in game, in practice, and even designing off field adaptations."

The 2021 champs, the Los Angeles Rams, may be part of that proof. The Rams are a team that believes in data and has invested in sports medicine and sports science as well as star players like Matthew Stafford, Aaron Donald, and bringing in players like Odell Beckham Jr. and Von Miller to help push them to a Super Bowl.

While the Rams keep what they're doing close to the vest, head coach Sean McVay has tipped his hand on what they do, including sleep tracking and a major change to their travel schedule, despite having some east coast trips that functionally put the players in game at 10am their local time. A change to their travel schedule allowed for better sleep, as McVay told Jourdan Rodrigue of *The Athletic*.

"Usually like my first couple years here, we would leave on a Friday for a Sunday 10 AM kickoff in our heads if we were traveling in a couple time zones. But what we learned last year is that additional night of sleep in their own bed, trying to keep as much of a normal rhythm and routine for the players was what we felt like was best, especially kind of learning more about your circadian rhythm and all those things. But I think the biggest thing is our guys get up, they're ready to go."

McCoy does caution that there are external factors that are often beyond the scope of even the best monitoring system, like what the Rams are doing. "I remember working with a college sports scientist and she was looking through all their data. She told me she couldn't understand why internal workload measurements were going up at the end of semesters, despite adjustments to practice and weight routines. The answer was they hadn't accounted for the stress of final exams and for the Adderall that many students were popping to get through studying for them!"

McCoy also warns that load is not the be-all, end-all measure for sports, even in the most sophisticated systems available today. "I have performance athlete checklist for sport," he explained. "One: the skeletal system is king. Two: the central nervous system management of the peripheral nervous system drives muscular contraction to elicit a technical motion. Third: the physiological system supports this workload through the delivery of oxygen and nutrients for cellular activity to create muscular contraction. Four: there is a waste production (expired gas) and the movement of non-oxygenated blood thats all a part of the physiological response to movement. Five: add in cooling regulation (sweat) and respiration change by oxygen demand and you've got a fairly complex system, but it operates and needs measurement."

McCoy finished our discussion on workload and tracking with something I found very interesting. "Metabolic load is not a load. You can look at it like that, but it's simply measuring the weight of the cart without acknowledging the size and power of the horse. We need something more, something better."

There's another issue, and that is whether the type of running that football players do is captured enough by simply measuring how much they run. An offensive tackle doesn't move much if he's doing his job! Most of the research on this is done in soccer and rugby, so it's not a perfect comp, but with both, there's more than simple running. There's a ball at times and there's definitely contact.

A landmark study was done in high-level sprinters, led by Pietro di Prampero of the University of Udinese (Italy) in 2005. The di Prampero study showed that the metabolic product was better predicted by assuming that instead of being flat-ground running, it was more comparable to an incline. This is easily recreated with a treadmill, so the question was correlating the metabolic product observed by positional data to the incline.

There's no reason to believe this wouldn't be the case in football, though we could not find any study that shows this has been tested. Indeed, the more physical nature of the collisions might make the theoretical incline more steep in football versus the other sports.

This suggests that there is a cost to not just a yard, but to every step, every action on a football field that must be countered by the body's ability to absorb that workload (i.e. conditioning) and recover in between plays and series. While a Derrick Henry type doesn't get better in the fourth quarter, his decline slope might be less, while his mass doesn't change, making his force feel larger when an opponent can't match him for either mass or acceleration.

Knowing what these values are and being able to calculate them in game could change how players are deployed. It would be the equivalent of having a battery gauge on players. The same could be true for players and knowing that information could lead to better personnel decisions, less injury, and better play on the field.

Companies like Catapult, Statsports, and GPEXE are working on advanced systems—lighter, more accurate, and even cheaper. While the NFL uses Zebra in game, the use of these other systems is near universal. The area where there's still asymmetry in 2022 is the interpretation and functional use of the data. Being able to tell a player or coach what the data says and how it factors into training and game plans is still underutilized.

Tom Myslinski is a former NFL lineman that went on to become a strength and conditioning coach for the Jacksonville Jaguars from 2012 to 2020. He saw the profession through multiple filters and in an era of rapid change. "[The Jaguars] were one of the first to use velocity-based training, one of the first to use GPS, one of the first to use a Nordbord, and one of the first to use force plates," he said. "The key was communication. We're a service industry as strength coaches. We have to serve the player, serve the team, and serve the coaches, all at once."

Myslinski was a co-author of a landmark study on the readiness cycle, one that's still being integrated into sport, but one that is absolutely a game-changer for many sports and likely for football as it gets more integrated. "We needed to know baseline numbers, so we could tell what state an athlete was in at any given time. Was it up or down? Was the load he was taking on what he needed to be ready, or was it taking it out of him? We used to have to do this by hand, guessing how long a route was and seeing how many times a guy ran it, but there are tools now," Myslinski explained.

While Myslinski still believes the keys are trust and relationships, as well as an athlete invested in improvement and accountability, he also believes that there are so many more tools available now that the profession is forced to specialize. This makes it tougher to get an holistic view and silos much of the key information. "I don't think you can be just a strength guy any more. There's no hammers in there, or not many. You need some dietician background, some sports science background, maybe even a physical therapy background," he said. "It used to be the more you could do the better, but it's more about the team you can put together now."

Yet again, this is an area where the NFL should be investing. Frankly, more research is being done at the collegiate level, an area where we could see some "bubble up" rather than trickle down. Football needs to get away from things like asking a player "how do you feel?" which seldom gets an honest answer in the uber-macho culture of the game. Instead, sports science could help the team know how its players feel at any given minute, in and out of the game.

Athlete Rehab

Until we get to a point where metabolic measures and optimal conditioning is universal, we're going to have injuries. The collision-based injuries can be reduced, but never to zero, which makes having medical staff and rehabilitation on hand for high-level football teams a must. While NFL and college teams do spend millions on this, in relative terms, medical staff and resources are cheap. Keeping a $30 million quarterback healthy or getting him back one week early makes sense on every level. Spending an extra million dollars to do this serves as a functional insurance policy, and can lead to wins or losses, which have real dollar values to teams.

It's an area Aaron Borgmann knows well. Borgmann has worked at all levels of football, including twelve years in the NFL with the Philadelphia Eagles and Kansas City Chiefs. He now works as a practitioner and consultant out of his own shop, Borgmann Rehab Solutions in Kansas City, where he works with all levels and sports.

Borgmann explained the difference in resources, personnel, and time, between a high school athlete and a professional athlete when it comes to their rehab. "I'm actually taking care of a bunch of ACLs right now. Time, money, resources—It's all a factor," he said. "I've got two athletes right now that are high-level lacrosse females. I see them once a week now, because they're at the nine-month mark. I'm educating them about what they can do on their own throughout this entire process is important for my sake, because I don't see them very often. That doesn't happen in the pros."

I asked if Borgmann could make a comparison between the pros and the lower levels. I asked, if the NFL is at a theoretical rating of 100, where are high schools or lower-level colleges? "Maybe 20 or 30," he responded. "That's just resources and time. It has nothing to do with the practitioners' ability. That has nothing to do with the athletes' drive. When was the last time you saw an Alter-G (an advance treadmill, which takes weight off a rehabbing athlete's legs and feet) or a Hydroworks (an underwater treadmill) in a high school athletic training room? That's day one, day two stuff for a lot of the stuff that we did in the pros. Forget all the fancy modalities, but even just that stuff changes timelines exponentially. Sure, some of the nicer high schools have pools, which are great or I get people in a YMCA pool sometimes, but just the the resources, the twenty-four-hour availability of people. They have weight rooms next to training rooms, and professional facilities. It's just easier."

Borgmann's work—and the work of those around the sport that do similar things—is almost always unseen. Most fans can't name their team's doctor or athletic trainer, let alone some of the rehab personnel or outside workers that help with the process. A few years back, an NFL athletic trainer said the most valuable thing for him that season had been that his team hired an assistant that did nothing but schedule medical appointments, MRIs, and such. That lack of visibility is often reflected in how people perceive the importance of this. Fans see a player hurt, hear he'll be back in weeks or months, and then barely think about him again until he gets close. All the hard work done by everyone is ignored.

Borgmann agreed with that. "With a professional athlete, you don't see the man hours and the time spent in the shadows. I would spend my days seeing players five times a day during the week—five rehab or treatment sessions a day, starting at 7 a.m., ending at 7 p.m. The actual man hours you're talking about is huge. Each player who's doing that is ten hours of work a day. That's not talking about people who were getting rehab work done at home rather than on-site, like a massage or even specialized equipment they have in their basement gym. That's one of the biggest things that people don't understand—professional athletes, they have genetics on their side, they have the best people at their side, but they also have time to do that more than other athletes. That's their job. If it were you and I doing it, we're going to be able to dedicate a couple hours a day at most. A high school athlete, college athlete, obviously, there's more time and resources, but I think it gets exponentially bigger, the more the stakes raise."

One issue often raised by athletes is that when they're injured and rehabbing, they're isolated from their teammates. While they vanish from the eyes of the public, often they vanish from the eyes of their teammates and coaches. They're not at practice and "out of sight, out of mind" is true. That can raise paranoia in a profession where everyone is constantly fighting either to replace someone or to not be replaced.

In addition, athletes can often be their own worst enemies. I asked Borgmann if he thought athletes were often the downfall of a rehab plan. "I've been very fortunate throughout my career to not have that come up very often. Let's be brutally honest—it does," he said. "The biggest pattern is that these guys and girls have never had to work very hard at being athletic. They're genetic freaks. They're gifted, they run fast, they jump high, they do whatever. Especially if it's their first major injury, it's a big deal. That can be a mental block."

Borgmann continued. "You get to this point where it's frustrating sometimes. [The player] can have a plateau, where it's time for me, the sports medicine guide, to rally the troops, provide encouragement, give them some small victories everyday, and get the rehab back on track. There's a big deal to the relationship and trust you have to have in a successful program."

One thing that has changed over the last few decades is the use of outside doctors, therapists, and physical trainers, like Bobby Stroupe. The paternalistic model is breaking down a bit as the athlete himself has become a business. There are often cases where it's not just the player and his family that's being supported, but an entire ecosystem that can include agents, marketing, a personal chef, a personal assistant, and can often include an entourage of friends and family that can be positive or negative, but all too often, very expensive.

I asked Borgmann if this change made it more difficult to do the job inside of a team context, or if he just had to work harder to keep it a holistic process. "I think over the course of time, everybody's always had people that they trust on the outside of the building. The NFL, in my experience, was no different than MLB and NBA, where there was a level of distrust at times between people that worked for teams, thinking we were trying to push people back on the field. I always told players that I want to make you look better. If you're playing better, or even just back playing, that reflects well on me. It was an issue for many players and many teams, because no matter what, if you couldn't get a player to trust you and trust the plan, it didn't matter. If you had an exercise or a process that was 100 percent effective, they weren't going to do it if they didn't trust you first. That was one of the very first things that we always tried to instill in people."

Borgmann continued, explaining how the circle that the team has to deal with has expanded. "The team physician actually does very, very little of the team surgeries anymore, as compared to fifteen or twenty years ago. The team physician sees people three or four times a week, when needed, but then X-rays and MRIs always get sent out automatically now, with cloud services to referring physicians and consulting physicians. Add in that those are usually done in consultation with agents." It's clearly a hard process to manage, adding more hours to the day that the medical staff is working. Add in the pressures of the win-loss record for the team and for contract status, and it's difficult at best, but NFL medical staffs get it done, time and again.

One reason is that by spending so much time and building so much trust, the process becomes a new way for an athlete to succeed. "Win the day" becomes more than a slogan. Borgmann told me a story about when he was with the Chiefs in 2014. That season had a high number of Achilles ruptures across the NFL—which remains unexplained—and the Chiefs had three of them.

"In 2014, I was with the Kansas City Chiefs, and we had a rash of Achilles ruptures. Within three weeks, we had three players tear their Achilles. Two different situations, game versus practice, two different surfaces, three different positions. There couldn't have been more of a variety. Two got mini-open PARS (a type of Achilles repair), one got a traditional repair," Borgmann said. "That experience to me encapsulated what I tried to be as a rehab professional. Yes, they all play football, but each one of those people had different demands. Each one of those people was a different body type. Each one of those people was a different personality. And yet they all had the same injury!

Borgmann continued. "I had to figure out how to make it all work. They all were expected back on the same timeline and they all happened in September. We had the whole season-plus to get them back. But we had them back in late February, early March, ready to go ready to practice again, and I was very proud of that. It was for a number of reasons, as I said, but mostly because of all the differences that they had with each other. There were a lot of sleepless nights there, you know, and I still carry those relationships with me."

You could hear the pride in Borgmann's voice as he went through the story, but there was something more, and his story took on even more meaning as he went through the names of those three players. "Mike DeVito, defensive lineman. Derek Johnson, a great linebacker, and one of my favorites. Then Joe McKnight, the running back and RIP" McKnight was killed just over a year later, shot in a road rage incident outside New Orleans. "He and I got to be really good buddies throughout that process. He was working his way back to the NFL when that happened. That holds a special place for me."

Borgmann's story of his three Achilles rehabs is a special one, but every NFL and high-level medical staffer around college has similar stories of success, of trust and relationships, and often, of dreams that didn't quite come true for a variety of reasons. When an athlete vanishes from the public eye during a rehab, he's not alone. The problem is that the professionals spending hours a day are never seen and seldom recognized. That should not be the case.

DRAFT

"With the first pick in the 2022 NFL Draft, the Jacksonville Jaguars select. . ."

There's a moment of pure anticipation before a player's name is called in the NFL draft. It's a coming-of-age moment for prospects who have worked their entire lives to make their dream of playing professionally a reality. It's a chance for general managers to find their team's next superstar. For fans, it's a moment of suspense before being delighted or outraged.

The NFL draft has become one of the biggest spectacles in the sport despite taking place in late April, months after the conclusion of the football season. The 2020 NFL Draft shattered its previous record for viewers, averaging an audience of 8.3 million people throughout the three-day event.

Those are staggering numbers for an event that involves thirty-two teams selecting more than 250 players over the course of three days. For reference, the NBA playoffs during the 2020–21 post-season heading into the Finals averaged just 3.7 million viewers, while the Finals that year averaged 9.89 million.

Roger Goodell and the NFL front office have successfully focused on marketing the draft as an event and traveling specta-cle. After the 2014 draft, the event has been hosted by Chicago, Philadelphia, Dallas, Nashville, Cleveland, and most recently Las Vegas. In 2019, more than 600,000 fans attended the event in person in Nashville.

For as much that has gone into turning the draft into a national event, it doesn't even compare to the time and resources put into into the pre-draft process. Players, coaches, general managers, scouts, trainers, agents, and media members work relentlessly to prepare for the event.

It isn't a groundbreaking statement to say that the best football players in the NFL are also world-class athletes. In order to play the game at a high level, a certain level of God-given athleticism is required.

However, the level at which that athleticism is measured is taken down to fractions of units by scouts to try and find which players will have even the slightest of edges on the field. At the NFL Scouting Combine in Indianapolis, speeds are measured down to the hundredth of a second, heights are measured to the eighth of an inch, and everything from hand size to vertical leaping ability is measured under immense scrutiny.

In many cases, these athletic and physical measurements can make or break the draft stock of a player. A great performance can elevate a prospect into the first round, much like Byron Jones was able to do in 2015 when he set the world record in the broad jump, leaping 12'3" while posting elite scores in other athletic tests throughout the weekend.

At the same time, a bad score in even a handful of drills can put a player under intense scrutiny from scouts and media members across the country. Former Ole Miss star receiver DK Metcalf experienced that coming out of college.

Metcalf was a high school All-American before attending the University of Mississippi, popularly known as Ole Miss.

At 6'4" and 230 pounds, he was an athletic mismatch that made it almost impossible for opposing defenses to guard him. In what was the highlight play of his college career, Metcalf hauled in a 75-yard touchdown against the undefeated Alabama Crimson Tide on the first play of the game, fighting through contact and sprinting past the defensive back.

Although his college career ended prematurely due to a neck injury, Metcalf's athleticism was well documented based on his on-field play. It wasn't until his workouts at the NFL Scouting Combine that a national debate arose regarding how athletic he really was.

Metcalf turned heads in some of his workouts, logging 27 reps in the 225-pound bench press while running the 40-yard dash in only 4.33 seconds. These were exceptionally rare numbers for wide receivers, but it was the agility drills where Metcalf struggled.

Where the former Ole Miss receiver put up historically good numbers in other drills, he put up historically bad ones in the shuttle and three-cone drills, finishing near the bottom in both drills among his fellow receivers. His three-cone drill time of 7.38 seconds put him in just the third percentile of receivers who had ever posted a time in the drill.

Debates over Metcalf's draft projection became a hot topic among national media outlets, with some of the largest platforms in sports media having wildly different opinions about the young receiver.

"Teams seek out pass catchers with rare height, weight, and speed dimensions, and Metcalf has those for days," Lance Zierlein of NFL.com said prior to the 2019 NFL draft.

"Metcalf's physical abilities are tantalizing," *Bleacher Report*'s Gary Davenport said. "Tempting. But he's a huge gamble. A casino game—one without especially favorable odds."

Not surprisingly, Metcalf wasn't thrilled with some of the comments labeling him as a future bust. In an interview with Jonathan Jones of *Sports Illustrated* in April 2019, Metcalf addressed concerns about his agility and questions on whether he was too big to play at the next level.

"Whoever has that question," Metcalf said, "come out and guard me, and you tell me if I'm too big to play receiver."

By the time the 2019 NFL Draft came around, the NFL still had its concerns about his agility scores from the combine. Eight wide receivers were taken ahead of him that weekend, and his name wasn't called until the 64th overall pick, when Seattle Seahawks general manager John Schneider and head coach Pete Carroll gave him a call.

It didn't take long for NFL teams to regret passing on Metcalf. In his first three NFL seasons, he became one of the league's most explosive playmakers at the position, catching 216 passes for 3,170 yards and 29 touchdowns.

No other receiver from the 2019 draft class had exceeded Metcalf's yards or touchdowns in their career through 2021. In fact, the four wide receivers taken immediately before Metcalf (Mecole Hardman, JJ Arcega-Whiteside, Parris Campbell, and Andy Isabella) had fewer combined catches, yards, and touchdowns than the Seahawks star receiver over that span.

Metcalf is a prime example of the importance of athletic profiles beyond the microscopic lens of one or two drills. Finding a way to quantify a player's athletic ability can be tricky when looking at multiple tests and scores, but Kent Lee Platte has created an aggregate score that has become the standard for media members trying to understand athleticism in draft prospects.

Platte is a lifelong Detroit Lions fan who started to get into writing about football prior to the 2009 NFL Draft, when the Lions selected Matthew Stafford with the first overall pick. It wasn't until 2012 that he started to become more interested in the data and metrics side of the game thanks to a debate surrounding running back Le'Veon Bell.

Bell was an outstanding running back at Michigan State and a first-team All-American in his final college season. However, after running the 40-yard dash in only 4.6 seconds during the pre-draft process, his athleticism was brought into question.

"The whole narrative for like three weeks was how unathletic he was," Platte told me. "But all of his other tests were really good, and it bothered me that the whole argument about his athleticism was centered around this average 40-yard dash time."

Platte then spent time focusing on the buzz words he heard surrounding Bell. Phrases he continually heard included "quick, but not fast," "he's a burner," and other commonly used phrases by national media outlets. He felt that none of these phrases were helpful or meaningful to understanding a player's athleticism, so he set out to find a metric that could do those things.

One of the other reasons Platte was interested in creating an athleticism metric was to give fans something that was more readily available than SPARQ, a company that created a standardized test for athleticism for high school athletes across multiple sports in the early 2000s. With their data not easily accessible or available, Kent wanted to create something that was.

The creation of the Relative Athletic Score, or RAS, started with Platte deciding to make the score on a zero-to-ten scale. He then color-coded the scores to make it even easier for the average fan to look through and comprehend.

"RAS is meant to be simple and easy to understand," Platte explained. "Because the average fan isn't going to know if a 4.53 is a good 40 time."

Platte admits that the first iteration of RAS was a disaster. Like any experiment, it took him constant revisions to get the formula to create an accurate representation of a player's athleticism. He mentioned that Byron Jones completely broke his original code after setting the broad jump world record back in 2015.

The formula for RAS was rewritten in 2017, where it has more or less stayed the same ever since aside from some minor tweaks. One of the bigger questions some RAS users had was how the 2020 NFL Draft impacted the formula and data.

With the concerns surrounding the global pandemic of COVID-19 at its peak in the spring of 2020, the NFL Scouting Combine was cancelled, causing prospects across the country to schedule pro days on campus rather than traveling to Indianapolis.

Surprisingly, Platte says that the data he received for the COVID-affected 2020 season and lack of combine measures didn't have much of an impact on his scores. "It messed up people's opinion of the data more than it messed up the data," he recalled.

The result of not having the combine wasn't inaccurate data, but rather fewer data points. Not all college programs share workout data publicly, whereas the NFL Combine featured 323 prospects from across the country with data all conveniently available online.

In previous years, Platte would collect both combine and pro day data for his database. He says that although he couldn't collect data on as many players in 2020, the data didn't appear out of the ordinary or skewed in any way.

"The data and scores I received were a little bit higher than average," Platte said about the 2020 draft process. "It wasn't that the data was bad, in general I don't think that we got bloated data at all, it was just that we weren't getting as much data on some of the more relatively unknown prospects."

The current RAS model treats athleticism roughly as a percentile of athleticism for players from both an aggregate and individual drill standpoint. For example, a player with a 7.78 RAS score at a certain drill would be roughly in the 77.8th percentile.

The scores from 0.0 to 10.0 are based on the player's position as well, so a 330-pound offensive lineman isn't being evaluated from

Relative Athletic Score
Providing simple context for player metrics on a 0 to 10 scale

D.K. Metcalf | WR | Mississippi

Hand-9.875	Arm-34.875	9.66		2019 RAS	@Mathbomb
Composite Size Grade :		Elite	Composite Speed Grade :		Elite
Metric	Mez	RAS	Metric	Mez	RAS
Height	6033	9.1	40 yd dash	4.33	9.9
Weight	228	9.76	20 split	2.53	9.66
Bench	27	9.97	10 split	1.48	9.93
Composite Explosion Grade :		Elite	Composite Agility Grade :		Very Poor
Vertical	40.5	9.7	Shuttle	4.5	1.11
Broad	1102	9.91	3-Cone	7.38	1.08

An example of a RAS card, courtesy of Kent Lee Platte and ras.football an athletic standpoint the same way as a 200-pound wide receiver is. Certain drills and workouts are weighed more heavily in the aggregate score over others depending on which position they play.

DK Metcalf is a prime example of not overvaluing agility scores with wide receivers. Using Platte's RAS model, Metcalf was still able to post a 9.66 RAS despite "very poor" agility scores.

One of the biggest surprises for Platte has been how closely his RAS scores have lined up with how certain NFL teams draft players at different positions. He cites that the Green Bay Packers, New Orleans Saints, and Philadelphia Eagles tend to fall in line with his scores, while he noticed another trend among the drafting of offensive linemen with the Packers, Eagles, and Indianapolis Colts.

"I am constantly asked if NFL teams are using RAS," he explained. "Every team is using their own system that they've either been utilizing or maintaining forever. RAS is merely a way for us on the outside to see and conceptualize what that might look like."

Although he has seen a lot of correlation to how teams draft compared to their athletic profiles, Platte acknowledges that it's difficult to try and make the same correlation between athleticism and NFL success.

"It's tough to separate the opportunity cost against the actual metrics that we're getting," Platte told me. "Testing well means you're more likely to be drafted higher, which means you're going to have more opportunity to see the field earlier and longer than guys who aren't drafted as high. "It's hard to separate that and isolate it as its own thing. In general, however, the best players in the league tend to test out the best athletically."

According to Platte, over half of Pro Bowlers at nearly every single position in the NFL have posted a RAS score of 8.0 or higher. Over 80 percent of Pro Bowlers at every position posted a score of at least 5.0.

"RAS is a better indicator that a player is unlikely to be successful if they have a poorer score than that they're going to be successful if they have a higher score."

RAS scores have started to be used widely by national media outlets to describe athleticism. Platte says that his website receives referrals consistently from platforms such as *USA Today* and *SB Nation*, while he has a working relationship with Pro Football Network, where he writes on NFL analytics and helps with their app development.

Platte is glad to see his work is easily digestible, so widely used, and that people enjoy sharing his RAS scorecards when discussing the athleticism of current, former, and future players. He plans to continue working on RAS while finding ways to expand, such as building out a tool to compare RAS scores of different athletes on his website, ras.football.

Although the data suggests otherwise, Platte does mention that he has a hard time believing that athleticism directly correlates with success at the quarterback position. He says that RAS scores do correlate similarly to draft projection and Pro Bowl data at other positions, but that it shouldn't be used as the primary focus in QB evaluation.

"If you're going to go draft a quarterback based on something like RAS," Platte said. "Then you're going to miss out on a very large chunk of the stuff that actually makes a quarterback successful."

Platte notes that it seems that there is a baseline requirement of athleticism that quarterbacks need to have to be successful but does not feel like RAS is the appropriate metric to evaluate the position.

There are dozens of factors that go into evaluating college quarterbacks, from passing accuracy to arm strength and mental processing. The pressure on NFL franchises to draft the right QB prospect is more intense than it is for any other position because of the value of the position.

Drafting the wrong quarterback, or even the right quarterback in the wrong situation, can have a damaging impact on an NFL team. Chicago Bears fans are all too familiar with this from the 2017 NFL Draft.

Heading into 2017, three quarterbacks were projected to go in the first round—Deshaun Watson, Patrick Mahomes, and Mitchell Trubisky. Watson had just led Clemson to a national championship, while Mahomes finished his final year at Texas Tech leading the FBS with 5,052 passing yards thanks to a strong arm.

However, it was Trubisky that ended up being the first quarterback taken. The Bears traded up from the third overall pick to take the North Carolina prospect second overall behind Texas A&M pass rusher Myles Garrett.

Trubisky didn't become the full-time starter for the Tar Heels until his junior year, but played well enough for forego his senior season and enter the 2017 NFL Draft. Although he didn't have the accolades and physical tools that Watson or Mahomes possessed, analysts and draft scouts were high on the junior quarterback.

"I've had Trubisky, my top-ranked QB, going as high as No. 2 to San Francisco in my mock drafts," ESPN's Mel Kiper said in his final big board of 2017. "He throws a nice ball, has some touch and velocity, and is mobile too." Kiper was correct regarding how high Trubisky could be selected, but the new Bears quarterback's career didn't exactly pan out how the team and fans might have hoped.

Trubisky played four seasons with the Bears, even making it into the Pro Bowl as an alternate after a strong 2018 season. However, he was never able to find the consistency that the Bears needed to take the next step as a franchise, and was unable to win a playoff game in two separate postseason appearances before leaving in free agency in 2021.

As if that wasn't difficult enough for Bears fans, Mahomes went on to become an MVP quarterback for the Kansas City Chiefs and led them to their second Super Bowl victory in franchise history in 2020. Prior to missing the entire 2021 season due to off-field issues, Watson had been a three-time Pro Bowler for the Houston Texans and as of 2022, when he was traded to the Cleveland Browns, holds the NFL record for career completion percentage (67.8 percent).

There are countless ways that NFL teams evaluate college quarterbacks. Film study, one-on-one interviews, and statistical analysis are just a few pieces of the puzzle for teams and scouts. While no statistic is perfect, Paul Noonan has developed a simple way to evaluate the position statistically.

Noonan is an expert in statistical analysis within both baseball and football. As an attorney focusing on a highly technical aspect of law, he also currently writes for *SB Nation*, covering the Milwaukee Brewers and Green Bay Packers.

Even before getting into writing, Noonan was an active supporter of analytics and advanced metrics in sports. He was a subscriber of *Baseball Prospectus*, a website covering sabermetrics, from the first day of its existence. He eventually spent a couple of years working for the website.

Because of his experience in both sports, Noonan wanted to find a way to compare quarterbacks and baseball players using statistical analysis. Given his experience with statistics, he began to wonder what the quarterback equivalent of "OPS," or on-base percentage plus slugging percentage, would be in football.

"OPS is honestly a crude baseball statistic," Noonan admits. "But the reason it's so widely used is that it's easily calculated, widely available, and easily sortable in a spreadsheet. I wanted to make something similar for football."

Instead of using at-bats, walks, and different types of hits (singles, home runs, etc.), Noonan used completion percentage and yards per completion to begin creating a QB version of OPS.

After inputting historical data into a spreadsheet, Noonan found the worst, best, and average metrics for his statistics so that he could create an even distribution of QBOPS scores that would scale similarly to the baseball statistic of OPS.

Despite its simplicity, QBOPS became an easy way to calculate and evaluate quarterback play. Noonan admits that there are other more sophisticated statistics like Completion Percentage Over Expected (CPOE) that are arguably better, but notes that QBOPS tends to track other statistics similarly while being much more openly available.

"One of the benefits of having any advanced stat is its availability," Noonan said. "If you can't easily work with the data, then it's not as useful. In football, a lot of the best stats are behind enormous paywalls that not everyone can afford."

With other advanced NFL stats becoming more widely available, particularly for quarterbacks, Noonan turned to utilizing QBOPS for college football. Advanced metrics at the college level are almost impossible to find and are rarely publicly available, simply because of the number of teams and the way different conferences operate.

While Power Five conferences such as the SEC and Big Ten may have the financial resources to track and publish advanced stats, smaller schools and conferences would have a hard time doing the same.

Because QBOPS is easy to calculate, Noonan had no problem creating yearly sortable spreadsheets of quarterback performances across college football. The names of the top college quarterbacks are easy enough to find, but QBOPS provides a way to evaluate which ones are NFL worthy.

Traditionally, there have been a couple of simple ways for NFL scouts to evaluate college quarterbacks, according to Noonan. The number of starts in college was an obvious one, as players who were good enough to beat out their teammates over multiple seasons were typically talented enough to play at a high level. The other traditional method was by completion percentage, with a QB completing more of their passes being considered a more accurate passer.

Advanced metrics like CPOE have been able to add context to evaluations, understanding that not every completed pass is treated equally. However, since CPOE isn't publicly available in college sports, Noonan's QBOPS has found other ways to add more context to evaluation.

One of the big ways QBOPS can evaluate college quarterbacks is by seeing how much help they get from their offensive systems and wide receivers. Although it doesn't traditionally track Yards After Catch (YAC), the statistic is able to screen out players who benefit from explosive offenses by finding players with middling completion percentages and eye-opening yards per completion numbers.

Noonan eventually discovered a natural threshold in his data for future NFL quarterbacks. Although there are some outliers, college quarterbacks with an "on-base percentage" of over .400 and a "slugging percentage" of over .600 tended to be successful pro prospects.

The 2012 NFL Draft class was a great showcase of Noonan's data. After eliminating small-school quarterbacks from his data that were outliers due to weaker competition, the remaining QBs to fit the .400/.600 threshold were the more successful players to go pro. Of the remaining quarterbacks, the following met Paul's thresholds, with their "slash line" showing their on-base (completion percentage), slugging (yards per completion), and QBOPS in order:

Nick Foles (Arizona)—.408/.721/1.129
Robert Griffin III (Baylor)—.427/.689/1.116
Case Keenum (Houston)—.419/.691/1.110
Andrew Luck (Stanford)—.421/.670/1.091
Matt Barkley (USC)—.407/.674/1.081
Russell Wilson (Wisconsin)—.430/.606/1.036

The list includes some impressive names. Although Andrew Luck and Robert Griffin III had careers derailed by injuries, they were the first and second overall selections in that year's draft class. Nick

Foles, who led the group in QBOPS, was selected 88th overall, but was the MVP of Super Bowl LII for the Philadelphia Eagles. Case Keenum went undrafted but has established himself as one of the more reliable backups in the NFL, playing for the Cleveland Browns as of the 2021 season.

Russell Wilson is perhaps the biggest name to appear on this list. Despite having an extremely efficient final college season at Wisconsin, the former Badgers QB was selected in the third round of the 2012 draft. As a great athlete from a prestigious program that met the usual QBOPS thresholds, he was overlooked due to his size.

"The only issue is his height," former NFL head coach Jon Gruden told the *Buffalo News* back in 2012. "If you just look at one inch, or an inch and a half, that's the height difference with Drew Brees. There are not a lot of quarterbacks who are under 6 feet who are playing in the NFL today or who have played the game, period."

Wilson has gone on to become one of the most efficient quarterbacks in NFL history. Along with being an eight-time Pro Bowler, Wilson helped lead the Seattle Seahawks to their first NFL championship with a 43–8 blowout win over the Denver Broncos in Super Bowl XLVIII.

Noonan admits that there are other factors at play in order to use QBOPS as an evaluation tool. Above all else, he still believes watching the film, particularly on relatively unknown quarterbacks that meet these thresholds, will give the average fan or scout a good idea on whether they're legitimate pro prospects.

"QBOPS can be a good tool to see who will succeed at the NFL level, but it still takes common sense," Noonan said. "A lot of this common sense is also common knowledge. For example, Ohio State quarterbacks tend to put up great numbers due to the offense and talent around them, but that doesn't always translate to NFL success."

It's not a surprise that QBOPS has ranked quarterbacks such as Joe Burrow and Mac Jones as having some of the highest all-time numbers, especially given them both being first-round picks with tons of talent around them in college. However, Noonan takes pride in finding overlooked players who meet the thresholds and the eye test to be successful at the next level.

For Noonan, the player that he will often bring up is Tyler Huntley.

Huntley was a three-year starter at the University of Utah, leading the team to back-to-back Pac-12 championship game appearances in 2018 and 2019. In his final season with the Utes, Huntley completed 73.1 percent of his passes for 3,092 yards, 19 touchdowns, and just four interceptions, leading his team to an 11–3 record while earning first-team All-Pac-12 honors.

Despite decent size, great athleticism, and production at a Power Five program, Huntley went undrafted in 2020. His QBOPS slash line also met Noonan's thresholds, going .431/.689/1.120, the third-highest number among all draft eligible QBs that year.

Noonan turned on the tape of Huntley heading into the 2020 NFL Draft and was impressed with what he saw, thinking that he at least had the necessary tools to get a chance at the next level.

"There wasn't a really good reason for why Huntley wasn't viewed as a good quarterback," Noonan said. "He wasn't careless with the ball, and he was making a lot of plays with good accuracy despite playing behind a struggling offensive line."

What was more impressive from Noonan's point of view was that Huntley had very little help around him to inflate his QBOPS numbers. Of his fellow offensive teammates, running back Zack Moss was the only one to be drafted that year, going 86th overall to the Buffalo Bills.

Noonan began writing about Huntley and his potential for *SB Nation*, but continued to see draft boards and profiles across the Internet that didn't have Huntley with a draftable grade. It was frustrating for Noonan, who saw the numbers and film from a quarterback he thought at least deserves a shot at the next level.

"It's hard to argue when you make up a stat that people should be paying attention to it," Noonan said. "But I was screaming from the rafters that he was vastly outperforming other prospects in simple statistical categories, and it was annoying to see him being overlooked for some no-good reasons, and maybe even some bad reasons."

Instead, Huntley went through the draft process without receiving an invite to the Senior Bowl or NFL Scouting Combine. His name was almost never mentioned across national media outlets, and he ended up signing with the Baltimore Ravens as an undrafted free agent shortly after the draft.

Serving as former MVP Lamar Jackson's backup, Huntley was finally able to showcase his talents at the NFL level in 2021. With Jackson sidelined for multiples games that year, Huntley was asked to be the starter in an offense that was built around one of the fastest QBs in NFL history. He ended up starting four games and playing in seven, completing 64.9 percent of his passes for 1,081 yards, three touchdowns, and four interceptions. He added another 294 yards and two scores on the ground as a runner.

Huntley's numbers weren't jaw-dropping by any means, but his ability to step into Baltimore's offense without the unit falling apart brings up questions as to how he went undrafted. It was amplified more by the poor backup quarterback play of that season, with backups Sean Mannion, Ian Book, Jordan Love, and Jake Fromm all looking incapable of helping their respective offenses move the ball down the field when unexpectedly forced into the starting lineup.

QBOPS and similar advanced statistics bring up legitimate and fair questions regarding how NFL scouts evaluate college talent. How much are analytics used in NFL front offices for scouting? Why do players like Tyler Huntley slip through the cracks?

Although Noonan doesn't possess any insider information about the league's front offices, he believes most of the analytics usage for scouts is based on athletic testing. He believes the consensus for scouts is that the numbers they get off their own charting data is going to be more useful that any data that is available to the public, and he thinks that can lead to players slipping through the cracks.

"Scouting departments start by picking players they like, then apply data and measurement filters to see which ones stand out," Noonan said. "I think they should consider doing the opposite as well, applying filters to the entire dataset to find guys to scout."

One of the biggest things Noonan notices from national media outlets is how rarely stats are used when talking about QB prospects. Instead, traits such as height and arm strength become preferable to talk about.

"That doesn't always make sense to me," Noonan said. "So much about quarterback play is between the ears, from processing speed to accuracy, and statistical analysis can still help scouts evaluate those traits."

The future of the NFL draft, and the game itself, will look much different in the future as teams begin to embrace analytics more widely across their organizations. However, media has embraced the analytics much more quickly than the NFL has done. That's the opposite of baseball, where "Moneyball" became viewed as a legitimate tactic to build a roster before media outlets were ready to accept the reality of what was going on.

The pre-draft process is still very much treated as a scientific endeavor, but teams are only scratching the surface of what's possible when evaluating future talent.

Not every college football player who goes through the pre-draft process goes straight to the NFL. Some go undrafted before signing on to a training camp roster as a free agent, while others never end up getting that chance. For others, the road to the NFL can take a very different path.

P. J. Walker was the starting quarterback at Temple University, starting the majority of games under center for the Owls from 2013 to 2016 under then head coach Matt Rhule. Although he never threw for more than 22 touchdowns in a season, he set the Temple school record for passing yards in a career by the time he graduated.

Listed at just 5'11", Walker was a long shot to play in the NFL due to his size and the fact that he played for a smaller program with limited production. He was able to sign on with the Indianapolis Colts as an undrafted free agent in 2017, but spent time on and off the practice squad until being released for good in August 2019.

Just when it seemed that Walker's football career might be over, the rebirth of the XFL gave him a second chance. He joined the Houston Roughnecks after the 2020 XFL draft, giving him another opportunity to showcase his talents.

Walker turned heads in his XFL debut, throwing four touchdowns in a 37–17 victory over the Los Angeles Wildcats. The season was ultimately cut short due to the COVID-19 pandemic, but Walker finished the year going 5–0 as Houston's starter, throwing for 1,338 yards and 15 touchdowns with only four interceptions.

With the XFL shuttering in 2020, many of the league's players were left without another opportunity to play football. For Walker, however, his former college coach, Matt Rhule, had become the head coach with the Carolina Panthers, and signed his former QB to a two-year deal in March 2020.

Although Walker hasn't taken the NFL by storm, his football career was able to continue thanks to the XFL. Spring football leagues like the XFL have had to be creative when scouring the country for pro-caliber talent, and people like Justis Mosqueda found ways to combine athletic testing and statistical analysis to help improve the league's overall on-field product.

Mosqueda got his start with *Bleacher Report* at only 19 years old, covering the NFL and evaluating players for the platform. Around the same time, he started working with Optimum Scouting, a consulting service for agents who represented players interested in declaring for the NFL draft.

It was at Optimum Scouting where Mosqueda met Eric Galko. After years of writing and working with various companies, he was approached by Galko about joining him again to help run personnel for the XFL. It didn't take long before Mosqueda suddenly became the No. 2 guy in the XFL's scouting department.

"Things ramped up really quick," Mosqueda said. "We wrote up literally hundreds of scouting reports on quarterbacks for the XFL and did countless pitches on players we liked."

Mosqueda was named the XFL's director of analytics, but he worked in a variety of different roles to help get the league off the ground. His responsibilities included evaluating players, generating scouting reports for head coach candidates, and working to get more than seven hundred players to attend XFL workouts.

Lacking the NFL's infrastructure and capital, Mosqueda and the XFL's personnel department didn't have the resources to fly out to games or workouts on a whim. They needed to be strategic with their scouting while operating on a tight budget.

"We started with analytics as a cost-saving measure, frankly," Mosqueda said. "When you can save Vince McMahon money, that looks good for you. We felt that we had developed an effective infrastructure to do that before the pandemic hit."

Mosqueda and his team embraced data to evaluate college players. Over the course of two years, they built an entire database to evaluate players from college, training camp players from NFL preseasons, and even players from the AAF, another spring league that had operated for one season in 2019.

The database included internally-created calculations and metrics to evaluate players. For example, when evaluating QBs, Mosqueda and his team would use factors like AY/A (adjusted yards per attempt) and time to throw while filtering out "non-NFL" plays to create their database of players and rank them accordingly.

However, Mosqueda notes that one of the bigger challenges when presenting this data to XFL coaches was trying to get them to buy into the evaluations. Most of the coaches in the league were of an older generation that wasn't always willing to embrace numbers and analytics, so they had to pivot in terms of how they presented such data.

"In order to have this data make sense to certain coaches, you have to make numbers not look like numbers," Mosqueda said. "We decided to implement a letter grade system, giving players a letter grade based on which percentile they fill in with our data."

When prepping for the XFL's draft, Mosqueda and Optimum Scouting discovered that the vast majority of players that they were going to get for the league were graded as an A, B, or C based off preseason analytics. The D or F players were guys the team wasn't going to need to spend time evaluating, simply because the number of higher-graded players that were likely to be released from NFL training camp rosters was enough to field players for the entire league.

Like most analytics usage in football, the grading system that Optimum Scouting used wasn't completely driven by numbers. Statistics and athletic testing data were used, but other things that required an "eye test" were also factored into the equation. One example Mosqueda described for the eye test was arm strength in quarterbacks.

"There is no good way to measure arm strength," he said. "We had to create our own rigid definition of arm strength, then go in and watch film on quarterbacks and grade their arm talent based off of what we saw."

Other examples Mosqueda mentioned were on-field speed for wide receivers and athleticism relative to size for offensive and defensive linemen. Contextualizing these qualities was important, but statistic-driven data wasn't realistic or effective in evaluating these kinds of qualities. Still, analytics played an important part of the evaluation process for Mosqueda, Optimum Scouting, and the XFL. With the budget constraints and limited resources, Justis described his team's use of analytics as a way to create a baseline and make sure that their eyes were in the right place.

"You can't have eyes everywhere for underclassmen in college," Mosqueda said. "We used numbers as a kind of baseline, then critically looked at the data when watching the players on film. It's fine if you don't agree with the player's baseline, but if that's the case then you better have a good reason why you feel that way."

Not every player outside of their baseline was a bust, however. One that Mosqueda gives as an example is Washington Commanders wide receiver Terry McLaurin, who was given a "D" in Optimum Scouting's evaluation database.

McLaurin was a tremendous athlete coming out of Ohio State, but his production in college was limited outside of an 11-touchdown season as a senior. Over his four-year college career, McLaurin only totaled 75 total receptions in 44 games played, averaging only 28.4 receiving yards per game.

While the statistical data went against McLaurin, the athleticism and "eye test" showed a talented pro-ready receiver. McLaurin ended up being taken in the third round of the 2019 NFL Draft and has since become Washington's top receiving threat with back-to-back seasons of over 1,000 yards.

Clean and consistent data, particularly with athletic testing, has made creating databases like Optimum Scouting's much easier to utilize. While today's athletes are completely different than they were decades ago, it's just as hard to compare athletic data simply because of the conditions older players tested in.

One example to showcase inconsistencies in athletic testing is Jerry Rice. Considered the greatest wide receiver of all time, Rice posted a 40-yard dash time of only 4.71 seconds. In 1985, the NFL Scouting Combine was held outdoors on a wet field at Arizona State University, where it rained two days during the event. Widely considered a disaster, the event was moved indoors to Indianapolis in

1987, where it has been held ever since, although there are rumored plans to move the event to different cities in the coming seasons.

"When dealing with such a large sample size of players over the course of years, we're tossing out data all the time," Justis said. "But data isn't always perfect."

Since staying in Indianapolis, the NFL Scouting Combine has been able to collect athletic testing data on draft prospects for decades, which has helped contextualize the data over time. Justis believes that this collection of data is a big reason why the NFL has been hesitant to remove certain drills in order to give scouts as much data as possible when evaluating players.

One of the big concerns with moving the Scouting Combine to different cities is losing that consistent data. "Playing surfaces matter to a certain extent," Justis said. "Everyone jokes about Ohio State players running a 38-yard dash downhill, but the context will be important with athletic testing if the venue changes in the coming years."

Much like the combine, the NFL Draft process continues to evolve. Combine workouts and pro days have existed for decades, but the way teams and scouts use this data has changed drastically in the modern football era. What NFL teams are doing to stay ahead of the curve in the draft process will continue to be a mystery to the public, however. Much like many aspects of the NFL, teams will keep their own internal processes as private as possible in order to maintain a competitive advantage.

That doesn't mean the casual football fan won't be able to understand in general how teams evaluate talent. The processes may be constantly changing, but there are those on the outside like Platte, Noonan, and Mosqueda who have found ways of their own to evaluate NFL draft prospects and stay in line with what teams are doing today.

ANALYTICS

"The analytics say to go for it!"

It's a phrase that NFL commentators have used ad nauseam over the last few years. When a team is faced with a tough decision on whether to go for it on fourth down, announcers will refer to "the analytics" to either support or bash the decision to keep the offense out on the field.

But what football fans might not realize is that calling a team's decision-making, cost-benefit analysis, statistical models, and algorithms "the analytics" is a detriment to the work that's being put in by staff members across the NFL.

Heading into the 2021 NFL season, there were nearly ninety staff members across the league's thirty-two teams with titles related to analytics. Those roles ranged from Sam Burgess working as a data analyst for the Jacksonville Jaguars to Brad Goldsberry working as the director of football analytics and research for the Chicago Bears.

The word *analytics* gets thrown around as an all-encompassing term to explain what these coaches and staff members are trying to do. However, each team goes about it differently. To put it simply, analytics is the process of discovering, interpreting, and explaining patterns in data.

Analytics are something that each professional (or collegiate) football team handles differently. In general terms, it's the use of historical data or statistical analysis in order to make decisions that rely less on emotion and more on objective data.

While baseball has become the gold standard for an analytically-driven approach to running a professional franchise in the United States, the NFL has started to find its own ways to embrace today's innovations in data and technology. The Philadelphia Eagles represent an inflection point for NFL teams beginning to accept the role of analytics.

Considered by many to be the most forward-thinking franchise during the late 2010s, the Philadelphia Eagles incorporated analytics into their decision-making thanks to Ryan Paganetti, a coaching assistant at the time who worked with the team's analytics department to help head coach Doug Pederson make data-informed decisions in real time.

Paganetti's role with the team was focused on game management decisions. Prior to the start of the season, Paganetti and the Eagles' analytics team created in-game charts to provide Pederson and his staff with statistical data on when to go for it on fourth down, when to call a timeout, when to challenge a play, and other game management situations, with the charts being slightly altered on a week-to-week basis based on the upcoming opponent.

The analytics that Paganetti provided weren't always met with open arms, however. In an interview with *Forbes* in August 2021, Paganetti admitted that there was some open confrontation after a moment in their Week Two game during the 2017 season against the Kansas City Chiefs.

Down 14 points late in that game, the Eagles scored a touchdown to cut the lead to eight. Prior to the extra-point attempt, Paganetti told Pederson that based on his own models for win probability, they should go for two to potentially cut the lead to six. If the two-point conversion failed, the Eagles could try to go for two again on a second touchdown. If the attempt succeeded, the Eagles could win the game rather than tie it with a touchdown and an extra point.

"I shared this information and I had several staff members, during the game, freaking out and borderline having a confrontation," Paganetti told *Forbes*. While the decision ultimately didn't matter in a 27–20 loss, Paganetti's reasoning after the game got Pederson to buy in.

By the end of the season, the Eagles had fully embraced using data and analytics to make real-time decisions. By the end of the year, the Eagles had taken down Tom Brady, Bill Belichick, and the historic New England Patriots despite having to make a postseason run with their backup quarterback, Nick Foles.

Paganetti's story might have been an uncommon one just a few years ago, but the previously-mentioned number of staff members dedicated to data and analytics is skyrocketing around the league. In fact, Paganetti is heading out of Philly to Jacksonville, where he'll reunite with Doug Pederson.

Not only are teams embracing the use of data, but fans have become fascinated by the process of analytics, and media outlets like NFL Network are beginning to tailor some of their coverage towards analytics as well. Cynthia Frelund has played a major role in analytics becoming more of a focal point in media.

Although her career didn't start in broadcasting, Frelund's journey has made her one of the biggest voices in the football analytics world. Frelund started out working in finance for the NFL. During her time in the league office, Frelund also worked closely with the NFL's competition committee, working side by side with Hall of Fame coaches.

When the 2011 NFL lockout happened, Frelund moved over to Disney, working in business development and strategy planning for a group of the company that worked on the acquisition of tech companies before eventually transitioning over to ESPN. She kept in touch with her analytics contacts, as well as coaches from the competition committee, while she eventually became *SportsCenter*'s predictive analytics analyst.

Around the time the Cleveland Browns hired Paul DePodesta, famous for his role with the "Moneyball" Oakland A's, to be their chief strategy officer in early 2016, ESPN began to talk more about how football teams and front offices utilized analytics on the air. It was Frelund's first experience on TV, and her time on the air continued to increase once DraftKings began sponsoring analytics-focused segments for ESPN.

In 2016, NFL Network approached Frelund about returning to

work on some analytics-driven content centered around football. With experience in investment banking and a master's degree in predictive analytics from Northwestern University, Frelund had been working with data analytics for more than a decade.

"I'm not a traditional broadcaster by any means," Frelund told me during our conversation. "But that was secondary to the content we were developing, which was focusing on what NFL teams are actually doing behind the scenes with data and analytics."

During her time on NFL Network, Frelund uses her own proprietary data models to discuss different aspects of the game, whether it's predicting the scores for certain matchups, determining the best quarterback prospect for a certain team in the NFL draft, or anything in between.

According to Frelund, her data models were originally created using historical data from the NFL along with computer vision, a field of artificial intelligence that the league used prior to Next Gen Stats to measure things such as the distance between players and the speed of a ball carrier. From there, Frelund used this data to create formulas for certain aspects of the game, such as defining a "pressure" from a pass rusher.

"It was a way to define these aspects of the game without having to rely on an eyeball," Frelund said. "And instead, more reliant on something that was unbiased."

In order to refine Frelund's data models, however, an eyeball was still required. Context still matters within football, and coaches will be quick to point out that not everything in the context of a single play or game can be quantified.

"There's no such thing as one magic bullet," Frelund said. "So the toolbox that I developed is actually taking into account some of the opinions of the coaches I knew, and I had them vet my models to make sure that they would be useful."

While most of Frelund's models focus on NFL data, she also uses her proprietary models to evaluate college prospects heading to the

NFL draft. She will even post her own analytics-based mock drafts on NFL.com, where she will focus exclusively on picks that will maximize a team's potential to win as many games the following season, rather than predicting what teams will do.

NFL scouts and front offices are constantly trying to evaluate college football prospects and project their ability at the next level. While that process is still far from an exact science, Frelund is able to evaluate trends such as speed from a 40-yard dash time compared to their actual on-field speed.

"We're trying to create more of a resume for these prospects by filling out more information and providing more data," Frelund said. "It's never going to be a replacement, but it's an additional tool for the toolbelt."

One of the bigger misconceptions regarding analytics in football is that they're completely divorced from the game that's being played on the field. For Frelund, it's important that her data models are the marriage of both. Handling the coding and technical aspects herself, Frelund has started to add more of the psychological components to the game into her data models over the last two or three years.

"I started looking for things like what happens on the very next play after a quarterback gets pressured?" Frelund said. "Does the coach call another pass, or do they run the ball? While I can't live in anyone's head and I'm not on the sideline, I'm trying to get to more of the behavioral statistics that could help."

By focusing on behavioral statistics and psychology, Frelund is trying to find a way to incorporate analytics into coaching and player decisions in the moment, as opposed to what Frelund calls "neutral brain" decisions that are strictly driven by data without context of the feeling of the game happening in the moment.

One thing that Frelund is curious about, but currently unable to create a model for, is fourth-down aggressiveness. Specifically, she's curious about the benefit of practicing going for it on fourth down in order to be mentally prepared when the situation occurs during a game.

"I've had players and coaches describe to me that it feels less risky when they know that they're going to go for it," Frelund said. "While I can't model out feelings, I can say that intuitively it makes sense to me."

Having worked for two of the largest sports media platforms in the world, Frelund is seeing analytics in football becoming more mainstream. However, that hasn't come without plenty of misconceptions about what goes into data analytics.

"It's funny because the most common thing fans are now familiar with is a broadcaster saying something like 'the analytics say to go for it,'" Frelund said. "The funny part is that I don't always agree, because there's no magic bullet that will tell coaches whether or not to go for it."

Frelund does strongly believe in using analytics to help with the decision-making process, but the context of a situation matters. An example that Frelund gives is Next Gen Stats appearing on a broadcast saying that a team's win probability goes up by "X percent" if they go for it on fourth down. Because that's not tangible and focuses only on historical data, it would be more helpful to explain the risks and rewards given the situation, and looking at the types of plays that could be most beneficial in that given point of the game.

A great way to do this could be by utilizing a decision matrix, showing how win probability changes if a team goes for it and succeeds, fails, or decides to bring the kicking or punting unit out. Ben Baldwin from *The Athletic* provides instant win probability to each significant fourth down decision on Twitter using his "4th down decision bot." Something similar could be beneficial on an NFL broadcast to help casual fans understand the impact of any potential fourth down decision.

It can still be difficult for analytically focused people like Frelund to get more old-school coaches, players, and fans to get on board, or even have a basic understanding of what analytics really are. To Frelund, analytics in football are a strategy crafted ahead of time using historical data as a reference point and adds in context of the game being played in the moment in order to give you a framework to make more "neutral" and educated decisions.

"It's not this magical computer that sits on the sideline and gives you all these immediate answers," Frelund said. "It helps create a framework and gives you a ton of data points. It's trying to keep a coach's brain neutral to help them come up with the best decisions possible."

While less progressive coaches may not be embracing analytics with as open of arms as some, fans are beginning to see its appeal thanks to the emergence of fantasy sports and the legalization of sports gambling in certain states.

In a world where "hot takes" tend to get the most attention online, Frelund believes that fans who are tired of the same debates and arguments have generated a demand for more analytics-driven content.

"I think we have really smart fans," Frelund said. "NFL fans have really impressed me with their ability to understand concepts like man vs zone defense. It's really great to have that kind of interest, and what that does is create demand for content that explains the 'why' behind everything and how the game is evolving."

The relationship between analytics and content, particularly with national media platforms like NFL Network, is likely to continue to grow in the coming years. Frelund admits that sports gambling has changed the landscape and future of broadcasting but believes that it only strengthens fan engagement and their desire for more focused content.

NFL Network and other networks are continuing to give fans more coverage on analytics, but the internet has been providing analytics-focused content in sports for decades.

One of the most popular analytics sites online for football fans is Football Outsiders. The website focuses primarily on advanced statistical analysis in the NFL, while also providing some content on college football, betting, and fantasy.

Aaron Schatz is the founder of Football Outsiders, but like many in his line of work, his path to becoming one of the most prominent voices in football analytics wasn't exactly traditional.

Schatz graduated with a degree in economics from Brown University before becoming a radio DJ and music director, spending five years with WBRU Providence and WKRO Daytona Beach. He spent time doing freelance music writing and market research before becoming the writer and producer of the Lycos 50.

Before Google, Lycos was a prominent search engine for people trying to access the internet in the 1990s. The Lycos 50 was a column by Schatz to highlight what kinds of places, people, and things that internet users were searching for online at a given time.

As a football fan, Schatz also grew up reading a lot of the work from Bill James, who wrote dozens of books on baseball statistics and history. James coined the term "sabermetrics" when discussing his use of statistical data to analyze and study the game of baseball. "I wondered why no one had done that for football," Schatz told me. "So I decided if no one was going to do it, then I would."

One of Schatz's original projects in the football space came when he was trying to prove Ron Borges from the *Boston Globe* wrong in 2002. After the New England Patriots had won the Super Bowl the year prior, the team fell short that year after finishing the season 9–7.

Borges argued that the Patriots weren't able to make it back to the playoffs because they had failed to establish the run. New England had finished the year 28th in rushing, averaging just 94.3 yards per game. Schatz thought this argument was odd, since Borges also mentioned the team he thought would win the Super Bowl that year was the Oakland Raiders, which ranked just 24th in rushing attempts all year.

"That didn't make sense to me," Schatz said. "If establishing the run is so important, why are you backing this team that never runs the ball?"

Inspired by this, Schatz started using an old Bill James method of cutting and pasting box scores, except importing them into Microsoft Excel. He ended up creating a database of every play from the 2002 season, and then did research to come to the conclusion that establishing the run is meaningless in the game of football.

"You don't win because you run, you run because you're winning," Schatz said.

Now that Schatz had successfully created an entire database of the 2002 NFL season, he wasn't quite sure what to do with it. He started taking away some ideas from a book called *The Hidden Game of Football*, where he was inspired to come up with a way to measure success rate.

It was here that Schatz came up with the concept of DVOA, or defense-adjusted value over average. By taking the success rates and comparing them to a baseline and adjusting them based off the opponent, the metric that would become a staple in advanced football discussions began to take shape.

Like anything rooted in analytics, DVOA is Schatz's attempt to add context to the game. The metric can be applied to teams, position units, or players, and measures both yardage and yardage towards a first down. As an example, five yards gained on third-and-4 are significantly more valuable than five yards gained on second-and-15.

Traditional NFL statistics are only concerned with net yardage, and league leaders in different categories are given the spotlight regardless of their efficiency, the situations in which their yards were generated, or the opponents that they were facing.

"Doing a better job of distributing credit for scoring points and winning games is the goal of DVOA," Schatz explains on his website, FootballOutsiders.com. "[It] breaks down every single play of the

NFL season, assigning each play a value based on both total yards and yards towards a first down . . . On first down, a play is considered a success if it gains 45 percent of needed yards; on second down, a play needs to gain 60 percent of needed yards; on third or fourth down, only gaining a new first down is considered success."

The actual formula for DVOA itself goes into much greater detail than this, but this is a more basic way to explain it. Using these success rates, adjusting them to the opponent, and normalizing it to find a league average are just part of how the metric is eventually created.

"The short version is that it takes every play and assigns it a success value based on the down and distance," Schatz said. "And then it compares it to a league-average baseline, which is adjusted based on the situation and opponent.

DVOA has done a good job at highlighting the league's best and worst teams.

While Football Outsiders continues to work to add databases of previous seasons, at the time of writing the site has calculated DVOA for all seasons from 1983 through 2021. In those thirty-nine seasons, the team with the best DVOA has won the Super Bowl fourteen times, while the team with the worst DVOA has been awarded the No. 1 overall pick in the following year's draft twenty times.

"I started to share [DVOA] with some friends on sports sites, and they didn't think there was going to be that much interest in it," Schatz said. "So I just decided to start my own website."

Football Outsiders officially launched in July 2003. The site began to attract attention rather quickly, and it wasn't long before Schatz started collaborating with major networks.

Through his work with Lycos, Schatz had connected with Royce Webb, who was the senior editor for ESPN's Page2, a former part of ESPN.com that featured several talented columnists. Webb invited Schatz to contribute to a weekly quarterback stats column, which he began writing for the company in 2004.

Less than a year later, FOX Sports approached Schatz to syndicate and write for their platform in 2005. By 2006, Football Outsiders was providing content for FOX Sports, AOL Sports FanHouse, and ESPN.

In 2007 Football Outsiders agreed to an exclusive partnership with ESPN Insider, now ESPN+, that has continued ever since. Schatz and his team regularly appear on their platforms to provide analytics-focused content, whether it's playoff odds or historical pieces.

Schatz also briefly appeared on a TV show for ESPN called *Numbers Never Lie* in 2011, working closely with Charissa Thompson and Michael Smith to provide a show that had hoped to go beyond the normal sports debates by using analytics. Unfortunately, the idea was quickly repurposed and became yet another debate show without an emphasis on data-driven arguments.

One of Schatz's biggest moments of his career was an appearance on *Late Night with Seth Meyers* in 2017. As an avid Pittsburgh Steelers fan, Meyers was a dedicated reader of Football Outsiders, and would reach out to Schatz via Twitter to ask questions about his favorite football team.

After a few conversations, Schatz asked Meyers if he would have any interest in having the Football Outsiders founder on the show. Although they were booked up for that year, Meyers got Schatz in touch with his booker, and eventually helped him land an appearance. "That was one of the most fun things I've ever done," Schatz said. "No question about it."

Schatz has always been looking for additional opportunities and media appearances to grow out Football Outsiders as well as his own personal brand. While he admits that may sound like selfishness, it's something he cares about deeply, and what his background is in.

"At the heart of things, I'm just an entertainer," Schatz said. "The way I used to entertain was by spinning records. Now the way I entertain is by giving them football knowledge that makes them smarter football fans, which makes them happy. I'm more an entertainer than I'm a research analyst, because the goal of my research is for it to entertain people."

According to Schatz, his ultimate goal for Football Outsiders has never been to change the way that NFL teams run their operations. Instead, it was to revolutionize the way that the league was covered. Indeed, many Football Outsiders alumni dot the major media landscape, including Doug Farrar of *USA Today*, Bill Barnwell of ESPN, Mike Tanier, formerly of the *New York Times* but back with Football Outsiders, and Will Carroll, one of the co-authors of this book.

"I appreciate all the people who are now in front offices who are reading Football Outsiders and other platforms," Schatz said. "But what I'm really proud of is how the way the game is being covered. Beat reports are so much smarter about the game now than they were twenty years ago. It is astonishing the difference."

While national media members may not always be well versed in the finer details of the game, Schatz points out just how many local reporters, including the local ESPN and The Athletic media members in all thirty-two NFL cities, have become experts in advanced statistics and film study. Even the newspapers with older and more established beat writers will often have a secondary reporter who is more focused on those other more detailed parts of the game.

"A lot of these guys do their own film study of the team they cover, and create their own metrics to inform their readers," Schatz said. "It's really dramatic how much the local coverage has improved in all of these local markets."

Local coverage in the NFL, and the way fans have consumed that content, hasn't drastically changed overnight, however. Even with his own traffic on Football Outsiders, Schatz says that the growth in his audience and number of readers has been gradual over the two decades that he's been operating.

In contrast, there has been a clear delineation in certain aspects of analytics being embraced by teams. The Philadelphia Eagles winning a Super Bowl after embracing analytics for fourth-down aggressiveness and other game management decisions led to a wider acceptance of analytics within organizations. For NFL fans, however, there has never been that moment in terms of the audience directly craving more content focused on analytics.

"There have always been people interested in what I've been doing from the very beginning," Schatz said. "But it's grown gradually over time."

As Cynthia Frelund mentioned earlier, the NFL is fortunate to have some very smart fans. While the demand for Schatz's content continues to grow, the popularity of fantasy football has made it a bit harder for him to capture the attention of casual football fans.

"Fans have gotten used to judging players based on how much they help fantasy teams win and lose, not how much they help real teams win and lose," Schatz explains on his website. "Typical fantasy scoring further skews things by counting the yard between the one and the goal line as 61 times more important than all the other yards on the field (each yard worth 0.1 points, a touchdown worth 6)."

The legalization of sports gambling is still relatively new at the time of speaking with Schatz, and he's unsure how much of an impact it will have long-term on his audience. Football fans who are gambling are interested in any kind of information to help them make their bets, so Schatz believes there's obviously some value there, but so far he has yet to see any concrete correlation between the legalization of betting and an uptick in traffic.

The future for Football Outsiders is still bright, regardless of the impact that the legalization of sports betting will have. The site is now part of a larger company called Champion Gaming, which is focused on providing data, advanced analytics, and expert content through several different platforms.

Along with plans for an expansion of their staff and plans for new statistics, Football Outsiders is also expanding its coverage of the NFL draft, using their advanced metrics to add onto the conversation of prospect evaluation.

"Other than that, it's always about getting new readers, and figuring out how to deliver them content that they enjoy," Schatz said. "That guiding principle never changes."

Where Frelund and Schatz have used analytics to deliver content to fans, Pro Football Focus has found a way to capture audiences with teams as well as fans.

Pro Football Focus, or PFF, is a sports analytics company founded by Neil Hornsby out of the United Kingdom. Originally a site for Hornsby and his staff to grade players with his own unique metrics, the company has exploded in the decade-plus since its founding.

The company continued to expand its staff of analysts and began providing data to a handful of NFL teams, agents, and media members. In 2014, *Sunday Night Football* commentator and former NFL wide receiver Cris Collinsworth bought a significant stake in the company to help PFF reach an even larger audience.

"What really impressed me," Collinsworth told Peter King in his Monday Morning Quarterback column in 2014, "Is the fact that 13 NFL teams have contracted with Pro Football Focus for their data. I mean, I have been around the NFL for over 30 years, I know how hard it is to get behind the wall of those teams. And they've got 13 teams to trust their data. That's huge."

Today, Pro Football Focus provides customized data and services to all thirty-two NFL teams, along with more than one hundred FBS college football programs. The company also provides subscription services for their grading and data for fans, along with media platform partnerships with the likes of ESPN and The Action Network.

PFF has also drastically increased its number of writers, analysts, and employees.

One of those employees is Eric Eager, vice president of research and development. Eager was a Division II tight end at Minnesota State University Moorhead, where he majored in mathematics. After graduating in 2008, Eager went on to get his PhD in mathematics at the University of Nebraska.

After attaining his PhD, Eager went into teaching, working as an associate professor in mathematics at the University of Wisconsin-La Crosse. He worked with the school for six years, but halfway through his time there he found an opportunity to start working for Pro Football Focus.

Eager's time at PFF started in 2015 with him doing data collection, writing, and consulting for the company. Eventually, it became clear that Eager's role, along with the company's data science team, needed to expand in order to handle their growing database.

"I consider [PFF's] data to be the 'what' of football," Eager said. "But I think that bringing in predictive models and quantitatively-minded people allowed us to better speculate on the 'so what' behind it. If something happens in a game, we want to be able to tell you what that means in the moment, and what that means for the future."

PFF eventually hired Eager full-time, and over the time that he's been with the company he's seen the data science team continue to grow. As VP of Research and Development, Eager works closely with all thirty-two NFL teams and more than one hundred college football programs. Eager provides data and builds tools for the teams that are contracted with PFF to help solve whatever problems that they might have. While some teams work with PFF solely to receive the data that the company provides for their own purposes, others will request tools and solutions to questions and problems that they might face.

One example that Eager brings up is the college football transfer portal. With hundreds of college athletes transferring each year and limited resources for teams to scout them all, Pro Football

Focus can provide data on college players to assist these schools in getting a better idea on which players could bring value to their respective programs. For the NFL, teams may ask for data and tools on free agents or draft prospects to give them a better picture on individual players.

Along with working with football teams, Eager also works on the content side, helping the company's content creators with custom-built tools to help them better utilize PFF's data to make their jobs as efficient as possible. He does some of his own writing for their website, PFF.com, as well.

While Pro Football Focus provides services to both subscribers and football teams, there is a distinct difference in the services that are offered to the two groups. According to Eager, football teams are provided with the "grainiest" and almost completely untouched version of the company's database, while consumers are given access to a more "rolled-up" version of the data. Subscribers are also given access to different tools and data models for sports betting and fantasy football, things that an NFL front office wouldn't be too concerned with.

For Eager, some of the most valuable data that the company can provide to teams and consumers is their player grades. The PFF grading system is used on a 0-100 scale, evaluating every player on every single snap of a football game. While traditional stats are solely results-driven, PFF's grades are meant to describe a player's "contribution to production" on any given play.

"The benefits of this style of grading are numerous," PFF's website explains about their grading system. "Taking every play into consideration allows for a larger sample size of data to tell the proper story rather than just a highlight reel of plays that we tend to remember, for better or worse. We also work to eliminate bias by not caring about the level of player who is being graded, so whether it's the best tackle in the league missing a block or one of the worst, the same grade is given."

With a team of more than six hundred analysts, PFF has this team review games from all available camera angles. For each given play, a player is assigned a grade from -2 to 2 in 0.5 increments, with 0 being considered average. After making slight adjustments and being reviewed by a senior analyst, the grades are then added up for the game and converted into the 0-100 scale.

"I think that our grades are as predictive as some of the best metrics out there," Eager said. "If a quarterback is really well supported by his offensive line and receivers, he's going to have a worse grade than another QB with similar production trying to do it on his own. I think there's a decent amount of context in those grades that we're providing."

PFF's grading system isn't without its critics. Because the grading is using qualitative criteria that is relying on human beings to grade games, it isn't based in pure quantitative analysis compared to a site like Football Outsiders.

"Oh yeah. We do [use PFF]. Again, as I said, it's subjective," Washington Commanders head coach Ron Rivera said in a 2021 radio interview on The Team 980. "So to me, you take it for what it is, with a grain of salt. For the most part, they're pretty good at it. They really are. I've got to give them their kudos. But, to be able to definitively say 'this is what happened,' sometimes it's not fair. Because I'll tell you right now, one of the things that's always gotten me, when I hear a guy may get beat for a vertical touchdown, the guy goes, 'Oh my gosh, I can't believe he got beat like that.' Well, he was to the outside, he was expecting inside help. Or he was inside expecting outside help. Those are things that you have to be careful of."

Eager believes that PFF's grades are criticized mostly due to fans being so accustomed to relying on traditional statistics to determine a player's performance. For example, a player who threw for 300 yards and three touchdowns may not have a great PFF grade, but that could be because of several throws that should have been intercepted but were dropped. On a traditional box score, players like those wouldn't show up.

"People remember the highlights," Eager said. "But they're not as likely to remember the play where there was a defensive holding call while the quarterback threw an interception on the opposite side of the field. We have somebody charting every single player, and whether the outcome of the play is good or bad, we're going to be charting and grading the process."

Eager also believes that a lot of the criticism of PFF comes from the fact that they've become one of the biggest analytics companies out there, and that their approach is so unique compared to that of some of the other analytics companies out there. "The first person through the wall is always the bloodiest," he said.

The fact that so many football teams at the pro and collegiate levels work with Pro Football Focus might have been unheard of just a couple of decades ago. While Eager believes that baseball and basketball are more receptive to analytics, he also thinks that the NFL, and football as a whole, is at the middle of an "acceptance" phase of embracing it. He also believes that there could eventually be a pulling back by some coaches.

"Football is a noisy game in that there are only 17 [regular season] games a year," Eager said. "So there are still going to be teams that win without doing things the most efficiently. With injuries and years where the 'elite' teams aren't as good, there are seasons where teams that may be considered sub-optimal can actually win."

Eager points out that it's harder for coaches and management to shy away from data in sports like basketball and baseball simply because of the number of games that are being played. When teams are playing 82 or 162 games in the regular season, there's a much larger sample size than in football. That, along with playoff rounds being played over a series of games rather than being sudden death, can have a big impact on results veering closer to what is expected according to analytics.

"I think the progress [of analytics] in football is going to be a little bit slower," Eager said. "Teams are always going to be chasing what succeeded recently and that may not always be the smartest thing."

While Eager also views Philadelphia's Super Bowl victory under Doug Pederson to be an inflection point in the rise of analytics in football, he also notes that it didn't completely change the game.

Despite analytics typically frowning upon the true value of running backs, the New England Patriots selected running back Sony Michel in the first round of the 2018 draft. after falling to the Eagles. They ended up winning the Super Bowl that same season, taking down the Los Angeles Rams 13–3 in a defensive battle.

Eager explains that while teams may embrace analytics in certain aspects of their operation, they're unlikely to utilize them in all aspects. He points to the Kansas City Chiefs, who despite utilizing analytics well in their play calling, tend to fall short on that end when it comes to game management and timeout usage.

The Chiefs also made a move typically frowned upon by analysts like Eager the offseason before the 2019 season, trading multiple draft picks (including a first-round selection) to the Seattle Seahawks for defensive end Frank Clark and then signing him to a premium five-year contract worth $105.5 million.

The trade ended up panning out for the Chiefs. Clark had eight sacks in the regular season, but turned it on in the playoffs, recording five sacks in three games to help the Chiefs win their first Super Bowl since 1970.

Clark hasn't had nearly the same impact since that Super Bowl run, however. Despite making the Pro Bowl in three straight seasons with the Chiefs, Clark had just 10.5 combined sacks in 2020 and 2021, posting PFF grades below 55.0 in back-to-back years.

"Clark has been a disaster for [the Chiefs], but their quarterback has been so good that it overcomes a multitude of sins," Eager said. "You can see the progress of analytics in the game, but then there are situations like these that make us forget."

The trickle-down impact of analytics has been felt across football. More than one hundred college football programs are contracted with PFF as of 2022, and there are sure to be more that embrace the usage of in-house analytics. Eager believes that there are likely also high school football programs that embrace analytics out of necessity to compete with more athletic programs.

"The difference in talent between the Detroit Lions and Los Angeles Rams isn't nearly as drastic as the difference between Vanderbilt and Alabama in the SEC," Eager said. "In the NFL you might use analytics to try to give yourself an edge, but in college or high school football you might need it just to get on the same playing field as other teams."

For fans who want to see analytics be embraced across all aspects of an organization, Eager encourages them to look to football teams with limited resources and talent, much like the Oakland Athletics in baseball.

The A's are widely considered the first professional American sports team to embrace analytics. Unable to afford or retain top-tier talent compared to the New York Yankees or Boston Red Sox, general manager Billy Beane worked with Paul DePodesta to use analytics and sabermetrics to help turn the team into a contender despite limited resources. Beane's willingness to embrace analytics led to Michael Lewis releasing the book *Moneyball: The Art of Winning an Unfair Game*. The book went on to become an Academy Award-nominated film in 2011.

"I think that lack of talent and resources is why you might start to see analytics more in college and high school," Eager said. "Availability of data is going to be the issue. The NFL has Next Gen Stats, and college football can have player tracking data, but how available that data can become will tell us how far analytics can expand."

Whether or not the data will be available at other levels of football, the future for PFF couldn't be brighter. In 2021, global technology investment firm Silver Lake purchased a minority stake in Pro Football Focus for $50 million, giving the company a nine-figure valuation. Silver Lake has around $88 billion in assets as of writing this, including a minority stake in Manchester City's holding company City Football Group, and a large investment in the sports retail company Fanatics.

"It's one of these extraordinary businesses that's been built by hand around the larger theme of data and analytics," Egon Durban, Silver Lake's co-CEO told *Bloomberg* in 2021. "Now, with fantasy and gambling, people are using this to make real decisions, and that's where it gets wildly compelling."

The investment was used by PFF to begin expanding into other sports, including soccer. As of 2021, the company has begun to provide player grades and advanced statistics for fans of Major League Soccer in the United States.

"From a business-to-business standpoint we want to offer our data to whatever teams to give them the best information to help them win," Eager said. "For the consumer, we just want people to fall in love with sports. If sports don't evolve and information doesn't grow, then it can get stale. We want the consumers of these sports, whether it's football, soccer, basketball, or whatever, we want that person to fall in love and stay in love with sports for as long as they can."

Despite some resistance and pushback along the way, analytics are becoming a key part of how football teams operate, how fans engage with the sport, and how media outlets are able to cover the game.

Because necessity breeds innovation, this could just be the beginning of a data revolution in the sport. Schatz and Football Outsiders have been operating for almost two decades, but the Philadelphia Eagles are only just starting to turn heads and have coaches begin to change their way of thinking as of 2018.

If Silicon Valley is starting to see real value in the use of analytics in football, then why aren't football teams embracing it with the same enthusiasm? Is it because a lot of the more tenured coaches, general managers, and owners in the league are used to the status quo? Are young coaches starting to turn the tide?

The Eagles were the first team to change the perception, and for someone picking this book up decades from now, teams like Philadelphia could be the norm rather than the exception. Until then, we can only hope that people like Frelund, Schatz, and Eager can continue to show us the true value of analytics in football.

BROADCAST/GAMBLING

The game of American football wasn't specifically designed for television, but if early TV executives had gotten together to design a perfect product for its model, they couldn't have done much better than what football has become. Certainly, television has molded the games in some ways, but a pre-television football game was much the same.

While baseball is often called "America's Pastime," football has clearly become America's game. There's very little uptake or playing of the game outside the United States, despite continued efforts to expand. In the world, soccer is king, but in the States, it's football. That's largely because it absolutely dominates on television.

The game as constructed is bursts of activity, with time between plays, perfect for replays, discussions, and debate. Halftime is set up for shows, highlights, or more debate. Commercials get perfect placement with timeouts, injuries, and any other break in the action.

We've seen tons of innovation in broadcast lead to innovation on the field. Imagine the game without game tape or film! That used to come from the team itself and in some case, still does, but the NFL itself will sell anyone their GamePass, which has included the "All-22" view, which is what coaches and scouts largely prefer. This type of film is available for most colleges and even high schools by the 2020s, often searchable by plays, situations, or players.

Instant replays, virtual down markers, multiple angles, sky cams, drones, and even helmet cams have been tried over the years as "new and better" has been the order of the day. This comes as broadcasters seek to make their telecast stand out in the market-place besides merely their announcers, despite the expensive rights fees they pay for exclusivity.

Here's one interesting note. I was asked why NFL referees, routinely miked-up and able to make detailed explanations about penalties, continue to use the old style of hand signals. The answer I got from an NFL broadcaster was "sports bars." That's right, a significant portion of games are watched at sports bars, where in many cases, the sound is turned off. Next time you see a ref grabbing his wrist for holding, raise your beer glass to him in thanks.

Back in the early 1970s when it was introduced, *Monday Night Football* was completely new as a concept. A single game, seen nationally, and scheduled to be one of the biggest games of the week, exploded at a time when 40 percent of the population regularly watched something on one of the three broadcast networks.

Over the years, it's fractionalized. Games in 2022 can be seen on a multitude of platforms, from the standard one or two games on broadcast, a cable-exclusive on Monday night, a streaming exclusive on Thursday, and the NFL's own Red Zone channel on Sundays, bouncing around the games to show all the touchdowns. For all this content and seven of the top ten rated programs of 2021, the NFL receives over $10 billon a year, just for the US rights. All of this is locked in until the year 2033.

This is to say nothing of all the surrounding programming. ESPN pays millions more, just to show highlights on *SportsCenter* and other football-specific shows. The NFL's partners that run the NFL Network pay over a billion dollars for their access and rights, allowing the NFL to have its own, 24/7 media arm with all sorts of discussion, including breaking news on its own clubs and controlling the media message about the league.

Amazon paid a billion dollars for the Thursday night game, the first that will be exclusively streamed and is a big part of Amazon's strategy to expand its digital content. They will launch two separate billion-dollar franchises at the same time—the NFL and *Lord of the Rings*. It will be interesting to see which is the better investment for the shopping giant.

If anyone might know where the seemingly fragmented NFL viewing office is going, it's Jon Klein. The TV executive who worked on *60 Minutes*, ran CNN, and is now a consultant on the Emmy-winning HBO drama *Succession*, is now focused on what he called "Media3," the media's version of the Web3 moniker many have given to metaverse-focused creations. From something like a concert inside of the video game Fortnite to the Netflix show *Drive To Survive*, credited with the rise of Formula One in the US, Klein thinks the fragmentation of the current media landscape is going to lead to something much more positive: personalization.

Klein believes that the most important thing is not the game; it's the tribe. "We really think of the broadcast as an excuse for a group of like-minded people to get together, people who are members of a tribe that they didn't even know existed, who share a common passion for or admiration for a particular athlete, team, or sport," he said via video conference. "I was inspired by watching my 20-year-old son watching sports. He doesn't really watch the game, the game is the excuse to have his hand on his phone, chatting with his friends, all giving each other a hard time, his bets, his fantasy, highlights, you name it, and the game is almost incidental. It really hit me when I started seeing him use sports in that way."

Standard broadcasts don't work the way audiences do. While they've worked to show more of the game or the game in different ways, it's normally just the game, beginning to end. The rise of alternative broadcasts, led by ESPN's experiments like the 2018 "Megacast" with several channels of different lineups for the College Football Championship game, or 2021's "ManningCast," featuring Peyton and Eli Manning, plus a series of guests that often barely touched on the game.

Klein thinks that's nice, a hybrid version for the networks that can afford a Manning—and they don't come cheap. Instead, Klein's own company, HANG, sets up the ability to do the same kind of thing, with high-quality guests like former NFL players, coaches, and celebrities.

"We sparked the idea: What other entertainment could you program around the game? If the game is the call to action, what's the action?" said Klein. "My partner Lorne Greene and I came up with this idea. Lorne has a streaming production company that works with the Apple Developers Conference and the G20 Summit and other Fortune 50 global entities. Very sophisticated technology. We just thought you could certainly put the athletes right in the palm of the fans' hands and that would be a blow-away experience!"

Klein thinks HANG is part of the first wave of Media3, the next generation of content delivery and context. "Media3 is all about the audience being part of the content. You're in the Fortnite game— that's you in there, right? You are the content. That's what makes it fun. There's your friend over there, and there's this stranger who's trying to kill you." With Fortnite positioning itself as entertainment rather than merely a video game, adding things like concerts and other planned events, it's not hard to see how this could shift from esports to sports.

"That's where all of this is today. TikTok is a good example of 'the audience is the content,'" Klein told me. "Cameo is that as well. Zoom calls for general content, whether that's business or just friends getting together. Nickelodeon's NFL coverage is the first attempt to do that in the sports space, but it's a bit more traditional in some ways and not traditional in others. HANG is in that tradition. I think that we're in a moment in time where nobody understands where all this goes. Just as when the first 2G networks came around. Nobody envisioned social media being born out of that. Right when the mobile web was hatched, nobody envisioned Snap as the result."

Everything from the ManningCast to HANG seems to rely on personality as the draw. While a Manning is very expensive, the lesser-known athletes or hosts also have to have their own draw. I asked Klein why such a basic medium—essentially the same as a video call between multiple participants—is so compelling.

Klein immediately reacted to the question with a smile and a pointed finger. "I'll tell you a funny story. When I was a much younger man, I was an executive in charge of *60 Minutes*, the most watched TV show in history. I asked the executive producer—the creator of the show, Don Hewitt, who was a broadcast genius. I finally got up the nerve to ask him one day, why *60 Minutes* is so visually dull. There's not any graphics. There's not much action footage or anything like that. It's mostly super closeups. He said, 'Oh, that's because TV is not a visual medium.' He said, if you walk into a Best Buy and they have all the TVs going when they have generic action footage, people just kind of walk past. As soon as a face shows up on the screen, people stop, because we're programmed as humans to engage with faces. And that stuck with me."

He continued. "The answer to your question, it's why personalities are 100 percent of the equation. Good personalities, bad personalities—it's the persona. That's so critical. That's why Facebook has that sense of engaging with other humans. For us in our model, on a business level, you've got to have compelling personalities. People who the audience wants to spend time with, but the definition of what that is, well, it's different for every member of the audience! We've all got the people who fascinate us and who we would stop and spend time or pay money to engage with and it is not one-size-fits-all. The Mannings are appealing to 1.9 million people per week, but we're a country of 320 something million people. They're not for everybody. They're not even for most people or even close to a plurality of people, right? Almost no personality is! The huge advantage of digital distribution is that you can be all things to all people, and you can discern over time who each member of the audience holds dear."

That combination of fractionalization and personalization is the so-called Long Tail of the Internet, as popularized by author Chris Anderson back in 2004. Klein gave me several examples, including how Netflix has grown by hyper-personalizing the viewing experience to each person, knowing not just what someone watches, but how they watch it, in terms of device/screen, how often someone pauses, what show they watch after a show, and much more. That can be creepy, leading to things like rumors of Facebook listening in to conversations, or it can be delightful, like Hulu suggesting a product you might not have thought to watch or known about. The successes of foreign shows like *Squid Game* and *Money Heist* show there's a strong flight to quality, even if someone doesn't speak the language or have a cultural connection. Again, this is tribalism by algorithm.

For the teams, leagues, and conferences, all this personalization and fractionalization threatens their biggest revenue source—rights fees. If Klein's idea is that the game isn't the content, but the excuse for people to gather and interact, either with each other or with something like a gambling or fantasy app, those stakeholders are in trouble and rights fees will go down. When asked if that means that teams themselves will want to do more things, like a smaller version of *Hard Knocks*, or their own team HANG where it's localized for an area or personalized for a team, Klein nodded.

"Yeah, they're going to want to involve the audience as much as possible. The whole field of sports documentaries has exploded, thanks to *The Last Dance* and *30 For 30*. That created a kind of intimacy with the athletes. *Hard Knocks* certainly does that. It will make you care that some rookie got cut or that a third stringer hurt himself and will be out. Media3 requires that if you're a team, you find a way for your fans to feel that they are part of it! There's many ways to do that, but I think that that trend is just going to continue. We have miked-up athletes now. The next step is going to be the AR and VR experience of sitting on the bench with them. That's just going to be expected by Gen Z audiences. They're going to reject any content that doesn't let them do that in some way, shape, or form. The audience has to be included."

Klein is also high on the concept of the metaverse for sports.

While it's extremely early days for the technology and even the concept as of this writing in 2022, it's clearly something that's coming. In the sports space, the uptake of new technologies is always different. It took several companies years to figure out streaming, while the NFL never did. Another shift is going to likely give the same results, often clearly tied to old revenue streams.

I asked Klein whether he thought the metaverse would be a win for teams and leagues, or if they'd stick to old metaphors in new spaces, like building a virtual stadium to watch some virtual version of the game, or whether they will come up with new experiences. "I think they'll do both," he answered. "It's a natural instinct to think about what the first websites look like. They look like newspapers, because they were created by the newspapers, but then they morphed as they learned what the form factors are and what the user experiences are. The first TV shows were radio broadcasts, right? Then they just eventually morphed into a more optimal experience. I think you'll see the same thing in the metaverse and, you know, people just try a lot of different approaches."

Klein's view on the near future of television sports is one of the more thoughtful. The hope is that both the current and future companies that will bring football to use will be as thoughtful, finding not just new, but better ways to deliver the product to the people that ultimately pay to keep football growing, despite all the issues. If they can get this part right, they're halfway to keeping football as the top entertainment, not just top sport, for the next wave of technology.

The Rise of Gambling

Here's the other half of that equation. Hand in hand with the changes in modern broadcasting, the NFL and college ranks were thrown by a sea change in sports gambling. While gambling had always been big business in two states (Nevada and New Jersey) and there was a huge underground economy of both friendly bets and darker bookies that always seemed to have a Joe Pesci-type collecting, things changed explosively in 2019.

A Supreme Court decision overturning a federal law called PASPA (Professional and Amateur Sports Protection Act) took away the carve-out for Nevada and New Jersey, making it possible for any state to open their doors for sports gambling. States had already seen how casinos could amp a tax base, being sold as education funders and job creators, but having this in place now made it even more possible for states to jump into the sports betting market.

But it was more than just casinos. The gambling doors didn't have to be open in a physical sense, locked into casino sports books. Instead, two companies had prepped the path with app-based games that transitioned directly into phone-focused gambling apps. FanDuel was founded by four Scottish-based friends who found a loophole allowing skill-based games to be played for money, even with PASPA in place. Shortly thereafter, DraftKings was founded in Boston and grew rapidly, largely because they were willing to push the envelope on which sports could be snuck through the loophole, like golf and auto racing.

(*Full disclosure: both authors worked at FanDuel, prior to the overturning of PASPA and the shift to sports gambling.*)

This book isn't a history of gambling and certainly not a how-to, but the money from gambling, gambling advertising, and sponsorships, as well as the engagement with fans that purportedly comes from having some "skin in the game" was a great fit for upper-level football. The NFL had been searching for ways to grow revenue, becoming more reliant on broadcast rights even as broadcast ratings went down. The NFL seemed immune, especially big events like the Super Bowl, but the fractured landscape is still an issue for them.

Where gambling and data mesh is an interesting area for football. Gamblers are notoriously information-hungry and often lead the pack in their analysis. If you don't think oddsmakers are good, just watch how lines are set and moved. More often than not, Vegas is a lot smarter than the average fan, which is why those casinos in Vegas are so fancy.

Then again, at the time of this writing in February of 2022, Draft Kings just announced that they expected to lose nearly a billion dollars during the year as costs continue to rise for them, including an expanded marketing effort. At some point, the gambling companies have to be profitable as well as cash positive.

There are even some calls for not only a federal framework, but for a federal takeover. In Norway, the state runs the lottery and controls sports betting. Instead of paying millions to executives, the Norwegian system supports their sports culture. According to Axios Sports, 64 percent of the revenue is redirected to sports teams, all the way down to the youth level, with another 18 percent going to cultural causes.

In America, the hope is that it just trickles down, both in revenue and in analysis. Fantasy players and gamblers work with elaborate data sets and have setups that rival large companies and even the casinos at times. Several groups of players are known to have pitched in and created systems that they use to help win overall, but they leverage that by playing cooperatively and in large volumes. That's not just a big bankroll, but a systematic methodology of how and why they bet across a broad spectrum. That's often shown that there are information asymmetries—things that some gamblers know, but that aren't equally shared.

Gambling became taboo in baseball and college basketball because gamblers found a weakness in the system. Poorly paid or amateur players could be bought and caused to act as their paymasters wanted. That's not how modern gamblers work, but information becomes the battleground. If they know of an injury earlier than someone else, they have the advantage. This is why in almost all sports, rosters are announced a certain period of time before the game. In the NFL, this is ninety minutes.

The NFL also has an official injury report. However, it's mis-named. The report, which comes out several times during the week and details which players have missed practice time and could miss the game, is simply about availability. The designations are strict and enforced; if a player is listed as doubtful, then that player might have a last minute return but the team needs to have that come out to be a nonparticipant the correct percentage of the time, both over the course of a season and multiple seasons. Fines have been levied.

Because of how quickly gambling has entered the scene, things haven't adjusted. While the Adam Schefters and Ian Rapoports of the world will often break stories, they tend to stay away from injuries, an area where the NFL gets very touchy. Knowing about an injury or just that a player isn't going to play for whatever reason, can mean millions in shifting bets and if that happens when someone has better information, by definition the playing field isn't level. If you don't think gamblers have their own inside sources—sources that are compensated well—then brush the sand out of your ears, ostrich.

The overlap between the kind of advanced data that teams can use and what would be most valuable to data-focused gamblers is almost complete. The data that can lead to wins and losses on the field often leads to monetary gains off the field and aside from sponsorships, there's not any crossover.

Which isn't to say it can't happen. A Black Sox or point-shaving kind of scandal isn't likely—Vegas is usually the first to find out, and there are shops that do nothing but look at gambling money flows to determine if something is leaking out that shouldn't be, if some sharp better is more than just sharp but has a real edge.

Then again, just days before deadline on this book in early March 2022, an NFL player was suspended for one year for gambling on football games. Calvin Ridley, a receiver for the Atlanta Falcons, was detected to have gambled on games in 2021. According to multiple reports, Ridley placed multi-game parlay bets, some involving the Falcons, using a Hard Rock Sportsbook app in Florida. The book detected it, reported it to the NFL's integrity provider, and an investigation was launched.

While Ridley was away from his team and appeared to have no inside information on the games, the fact is that the rules clearly stated no betting on football. It doesn't matter if Ridley won or lost, bet for or against his teams, or the amount; merely doing it is against the rules.

Yes, there's cries of hypocrisy from some corners, but a rule is a rule and Ridley broke it. The NFL can have both "official gambling partners" and rules against its own players gambling. If anything, catching Ridley via the book self-reporting and the "integrity monitoring system" should create some trust in the system itself. If people wonder if the games are rigged, they stop gambling (or should). There's no betting on Wrestlemania.

In 2022, there's still some question about which one of these sides—teams or gamblers—has the information advantage. On one side, the teams do not cooperate on much, so there's a lot of re-inventing the wheel or smaller data sets to learn from. On the other side, gamblers are held back by odds, lines, and risk profiles, so even having the information advantage doesn't always translate into winning.

By the time you are reading this book, that battle may have been decided, but it is likely to take the better part of a decade, especially if there's no federal law that standardizes gambling across the United States.

The next step is going to be real-time gambling, or what some call micro-betting. This is nothing more than an extremely short-term bet with smaller amounts. The easiest example of this is predicting the next play. It could be the simple run-pass, or a more complex "run to right," "pass to Kupp," or something even more granular or unlikely, such as a score-on-play bet. There are also parlays on this ("pick the next three plays") that can increase the odds.

This kind of real-time activity feeds off precisely the kind of numbers that teams long have used to call plays. If Sean McVay usually calls a run to the strong side on second-and-short, does he play to that strength, or go against his tendency to try and fool the defense? Both team and gambler are aligned here.

It doesn't take much thought to think where this could go black hat. A gambler could get access to communication, or more simply, learn the team's play calls or signals. While they might not be able to find a player willing to give information, a couple hundred bucks to a ball boy or intern might get them exactly what they want. (Downside? Teams often change this from week to week, because they know other teams try to do the same, or at least decode what they do.)

There's a flip side to this as well. Not only would things like play tendencies, individual and team strengths, and other data from sources like Pro Football Focus and Football Outsiders come screaming to the fore, there's great incentive to find even more granular measures. Some of the inside data from teams might need to come to the outside, with gambling groups controlling some of their own data, likely with camera systems.

There's also some "wisdom of the crowds" data that could come back to teams. We'd learn which teams and/or coaches are the most predictable pretty quickly, and the adjustments that should come should reach some sort of equilibrium, though constantly changing coaching staffs would create data inequity early in seasons, unless someone figures out how to get hold of playbooks or inside data on installations in training camp.

The cat and mouse game is nearly infinite, so it comes down to ingenuity and incentives. Teams want to win and will do whatever they can within the bounds of the rules—stretching them sometimes, but seldom outright breaking them. Think about the last few "scandals" in football. Tom Brady deflated the football to get a better grip. The Patriots were caught videotaping a practice. That's about it. Advantage? Sure, but how much?

On the gambling side, the rules aren't always so clear. The incentives are.

The Rise of the Virtual

One of the key future technologies for the world, including sports, is virtual reality. I know, this has been said for better than a decade now, but the promise of the technology is finally getting to a usable state. NFL teams are working to use this to their advantage.

One of the key technologies being used is called STRIVR. Born out of the Stanford tech hub, STRIVR uses virtual reality headsets paired with pre-made video that allows a coach to actually see what the quarterback sees and to train reads. The technology has been quarterback-focused, but we're seeing some expansion of this to other positions.

At the same time, the company barely presents itself as a football tool anymore. The company has pivoted to business uses, including training and conferences. The football market is a small one and even the places that have the money and floor space to buy something like a STRIVR unit often simply don't (and when they do, they seldom pay full price.) Instead of showing the 49ers, Bears, and Clemson, STRIVR is moving more into the space where the logos of Verizon and Walmart mean more for their business.

While smaller companies have struggled to make a business sustainable, is it possible that some of the biggest in the world could succeed. Facebook changed its corporate name to "Meta" as they made a philosophical shift to where their business is going. Use of their current and future solutions, as STRIVR does with the consumer-based Quest unit, would be easy for football, altering units to their own purposes rather than having higher-end custom solutions that can't trickle down.

There are also other solutions that don't fit in the standard definition of virtual reality, but are more of a new visualization that can allow coaches to see new things on video. One solution being used takes positional data, knowledge of the athletes, and creates a video game-like setup. Canon, a company long known for its professional cameras, has teamed up with several sports franchises to create these kind of 3-D virtual worlds, where data can be drawn up into a near-real form in just seconds.

The system isn't cheap or portable, involving more than one hundred cameras in most setups, plus dedicated computer systems that can render the graphics in real time. Rather than a single camera angle, a coach could place his perspective as that of the middle linebacker looking across at the quarterback. A QB coach could track back to see what the quarterback could see, or perhaps why he didn't spot an open receiver or a crouching corner that's about to cause a pick-six.

The same technology can be used for training. One NFL team acknowledged using the system at their practice facility in a test, with the hope that they would be able to make quicker installs of new plays. The thought is that younger players are used to video game-type displays and allowing them to see replays would allow them to make spatial changes more quickly. It remains to be seen if that holds true.

We've already seen some systems installed that are less capable. Intel has a system that is used in broadcasts that create a 360-degree picture that can be "spun" from view to view, allowing both broadcasts and coaches to get a look at different angles of a play.

There's also the hope that systems like this, or even augmented reality—where a view of the world is standard, through clear glasses or re-projected onto a screen, but with additional features like data or identification added. An NFL defensive coordinator I spoke with at the NFL Combine said he'd seen a system that week that did augmented reality for personnel. Basically he could look out through "big thick glasses," not unlike the latest version of Microsoft's HoloLens, and whatever player he focused on, he'd see that player flagged with name, position, and other data. "Mostly, I could see who's on the field. Do we change the play when they're in nickel or if I see the run stopper back in the package? That could be valuable, but is it better than having spotters in the press box?"

This is an area of change that goes well beyond the on-field uses and creates a challenge for football in the future. One of the biggest problems that football has going into the next decade is the biggest advantage it had for the last twenty-five years. Here in 2022, the release of an NFL-licenced VR game, with Sony and Meta, drew giggles at a trailer that looks so limited as to be useless or at least not very realistic. Simply put, as the game was seemingly designed for television and then video games, it is not as well-suited for virtual reality gaming.

While it's easy to replicate a playbook and how to truck-stick a linebacker, or even figuring out how to record John Madden saying all sorts of John Madden things, no one's figured out how to be a virtual quarterback and take a blindside hit. Small mercies, probably. We're not even at a stage where someone besides Mark Zuckerberg has a room big enough to run around without knocking things over.

What gaming companies will have to do is find facets of football that can be done stationary. While I asked several companies in the sports gaming space, such as Electronic Arts and Activision Blizzard for comment, none would discuss future plans for competitive reasons. One source within that industry thinks it will come down to a couple things—first, play calling, which is the heart of modern football video games. That could remain the same, with perspective changes from the standard "TV view" to go "inside" a player's POV.

The other key, according to a source with knowledge of several VR projects that are in development, thinks that a QB simulator is possible. "It's not going to be perfect. It's stationary, pocket passer kind of thing, so expect Tom Brady to be the model," she said. "The problem is in five years, ten years, is that even a thing? Is every quarterback moving like [Patrick] Mahomes and [Kyler] Murray?" Simulated hits could happen with haptic feedback, but are more a "penalty buzz" than the shock and injury risk a real quarterback faces.

"There's just no way to do it and for most, it would be so uncomfortable you wouldn't want to [simulate a hit]," she explained. "Haptics are getting better. A shock is what you want, a big bass thump rather than Aaron Donald knocking someone into next week."

That's all correct, and interesting, but as virtual reality becomes more and more real, there's an "uncanny valley" that happens when something that looks and sounds real doesn't feel real. That immersion can happen for stationary sports like baseball and golf, but motion and contact makes it tougher for the next hit to be Madden, FIFA, or NBA 2K.

There's so many technologies on the way that it's difficult to imagine just how an NFL broadcast—or streaming, or metaverse, or virtual experience—will look in the not too distant future. The changes will upset football at all levels, disrupting the comfort and income stream that everyone from the NFL to Friday night high school football has received from the rights fees and ad-supported half-century.

THE FUTURE OF FOOTBALL

From time to time, people will say that American football will just fade away. It's faced these crises more than once, from Teddy Roosevelt to Donald Trump (who attempted to sue his way into the NFL), from concussions to dropping youth participation, and all those times when people said that *other* football would fast take over once America decided to join the rest of the world. American football is not without challenges, but it's safe to say it's more likely to make it another century than fade out before then.

It's also more likely than not that the game in twenty years, even fifty years, looks more similar to the current game than not. If we go back fifty years, there are plenty of changes, but the game is recognizable. A few of the stadiums are still in use.

If you ask people around football, the future seems to be filled with fear. For a league with such a powerful position and one that seems to be consolidating, even in a changing world, that's surprising.

Fans seem to worry about a watering down of their game. For many, that's a fear of expansion reducing the talent level, of soccer taking over and taking some of the best players, or for a reduction in the sheer violence of the game. Fans, when asked on Twitter, overwhelmingly said that they thought football in twenty years would either be flag football or that the game would be feminized, often in exactly those terms. Misogyny aside, there's little logic in this.

Football has taken steps to limit risk, injury, and also the violence and brutality of the game. However, football today and football twenty years ago look very much the same despite this.

Some believe that instead of being feminized or reduced, the game's real danger is that it could be dehumanized. Fox has used

"Cleatus," a football robot, as their mascot during coverage for better than a decade. He's animated and even the wildest dreams of Elon Musk in 2022 don't have anything like this on the near horizon. (This is one sentence we hope is really wrong ten years from now . . . and beyond!)

If there's any real danger to football, it's far more subtle. Football is so reliant on standard linear television that the impending demise of this and a shift to a streaming or direct-to-consumer model has great financial risk.

Even this is muted, by the sheer scale of the game and the league. Both the NFL and major colleges could lose half their revenue. Yet the salary cap comes down, players adjust, and the game moves forward. Even for players, this wouldn't be a disaster. Costly, yes, but there are new models for making money and extending careers beyond the playing field.

A bigger danger is the loss of the feeder system. There were worries at the height of the concussion crisis that mothers would be the real problem. If moms around the US decided youth football wasn't safe for the brains of their sons and daughters, the funnel of talent that narrows to the elite levels gets less material to work with year over year and that reduction, like a birth rate, is key to the game. Even while athletes continue to get bigger, faster, and stronger, what the game couldn't handle is those athletes being lesser.

The NFL could do more to protect against this. It needs to continue making the game safer, but still showing action enough to protect its ratings and to inspire the same youth it needs playing the game. More safety initiatives will help, but the biggest would be to reduce or at least subsidize the cost of the game.

Part of that might be a big change. 7-on-7 football is a huge growth area and has been adopted by developmental and prospect leagues. It entails less equipment, fewer players, and fewer injuries (but not injury-free.) Shifting this to lower levels would be a big step, while still allowing skill-building time for the 11-on-11 game that's well known.

Even helping with grants for high schools, especially outside the strongest areas—Florida, Texas, and California—would prove to be of great value. The distribution of the game has always been southern, so shifting that up slightly and getting more urban areas would increase the funnel.

One answer to a lot of the NFL's problems is the current push for international expansion. The NFL could get more eyeballs, more tickets, and more players this way. While the game has some popularity overseas, they have almost no involvement. There have been players from more than twenty countries in the NFL, but most were conversions from rugby or soccer, physical freaks that came to the US for college and tried the sport, or some similar unusual path story.

In 2021, the NFL set up a structure of "exclusive rights territories" that teams were allowed to bid on. There's not a lot of details about what these rights entail, but allowing any team to have just exclusive marketing rights in a territory could unlock a cash flow. If the LA Rams, a team that was active in that auction, could hold games in Mexico, Germany, and southeast Asia, we might see more interest in the sport in areas that are mixed. It's one of few areas where individual teams, rather than the league as a whole, have an opportunity.

Beyond this, we've seen both NFL and college games in the United Kingdom, Ireland, Germany, and Mexico in the last decade. It's hard to imagine that they won't try in France, Spain, Italy, Brazil, or China. While the latter has some human rights issues, anywhere with a soccer stadium is a potential host for an NFL game. Rather than a threat, most have seen it like a concert—a chance to get fans in the stand for a one-off event. Add in that there's significant ownership crossover with the NFL and international soccer, a two-way relationship could end up working for all.

In fact, this "summer soccer league" has been discussed, with as many as ten teams holding summer exhibitions in NFL stadiums and training camps. Manchester United could play in Tampa, given that the Glazer family owns both. Liverpool could play in Boston, or LeBron James could put them in Los Angeles, Cleveland, or both. Man City could pair up with NYCFC in Yankee Stadium, at least until their new soccer-only stadium is built.

For the NFL, to team up with some of the bigger soccer clubs, especially ones that already have ties to existing NFL owners, gives them access into growing the game globally, both in terms of fans, mind share, and the all-important video rights, however they exist over the next ten years.

The global expansion is not likely to increase the feeder system. There will still be the occasional talent that decides to put on a helmet, but that's part of the problem. Soccer and basketball need a ball and a goal and not much more, while American football needs much more equipment, even if it can be played, more or less, on a soccer pitch.

That's where the rise of 7-on-7 football may see its most growth. While developed as a skill-position development game without the contact, the version inadvertently made the game more accessible to the world. In places where rugby or soccer rule, there's always the chance that secondary players might convert for more chance to play or to play off singular skills like speed (or a lack of skills necessary for the others!).

As in the US, this is yet another area where subsidies could help, especially if paired with local games. Germany, Mexico, and Africa are key areas for this, and all could see NFL games during the first half of the 2020s.

Advances in equipment should continue, but are likely to remain evolutionary. Unfortunately, there's been no great leap forward in a while on any front. The same is true for injury management. While there's hope of reducing injuries and rehab times, football is more reliant on general medical research than driving it by itself. Even the NFL is a very small market for this and it's more likely to trickle down from things like advances in geriatric joint management than from the game itself.

All in all, it would be no surprise to see football in ten, twenty, even fifty years looking more or less like it did ten, twenty, or even fifty years ago. We may dream of flying cars and jetpacks, but football's advances are likely to be much the same, falling far short of what the futurists expected.

That's not to say that the game is in any sort of crisis. While it's impossible to expect the game will continue to see a rise in revenue at the recent pace, even with international expansion, the game could safely deal with revenue contraction if necessary. There's no indication that football, specifically NFL football, will cease being the most desired and watched content in America. That gives them wide berth to add to it until there's some sign of glut, something we simply haven't seen yet.

There may be no business in the world that seems better positioned for the future than the NFL and absent major changes, that's only going to get even stronger. The NFL has overcome recession, war, and its own internal crises before and whatever comes in the future is likely to challenge it, but see the NFL shield come out on top again.

The future of football is bright, a generational concern that can feed both the body and the mind, as well as fill the wallets of the talented players and coaches, and the rich owners behind the scenes. Hopefully, as they fill their wallets, they continue to follow the science and make the game smarter, safer, and better for those that come after.

ACKNOWLEDGMENTS

Will Carroll would like to acknowledge everyone at Skyhorse Publishing, especially Julie Ganz. Special thanks to Jimbo Fisher, Dr. Chad Lavender, Dr. Neal ElAttrache, Dennis Allen, Cory Alexander, Stephen Wolfram, Hugh Douglas, Abe Gordon, John Fricke, Gary McCoy, Jon Klein, Kayla Ibe, Gina Amoroso, Bobby Stroupe, Aaron Borgmann, Tom Myslinski, Matt Sheldon, Tim Gabbett, Steve Koers, and Peter King.

Tyler Brooke would like to acknowledge and thank Julie Ganz, everyone else at Skyhorse Publishing, Calle Emanuelsson, Nick Banas, Andrew Howard, Joe Thomas, Kevin Kelley, Doug Farrar, Mark Schofield, Steve Schuh, Dr. Michael Sonne, Kent Lee Platte, Paul Noonan, Justis Mosqueda, Sam Schwartzstein, Adam Shunk, Cynthia Frelund, Aaron Schatz, Eric Eager, and Peter King.

As with *The Science of Baseball*, this book couldn't have been completed without the assistance of David Barshop. He's an invaluable resource and he deserves a lot of credit.

Chicago style is used in this book, which states that professional titles are not capitalized. For members of the NATA out there, please note.

Parts of this book were based on works previously published by the authors. In the section on Dr. Chad Lavender and ACLs, it was previously published at the *Under The Knife* newsletter. The section on heat illness contains material previously published at Baseball Prospectus.

In this book, we regularly use the masculine form in references, due to the overwhelming majority of players at all levels currently being male. This is in no way a slight to the women who choose to play or efforts to expand the game to more female opportunity, on and off the field.